THE 100+ SERIES™

Reproducible Activities

Standards-Based
Math

Grades 7-8

By
Harold Torrance

Cover Design by
Jeff Van Kanegan

Published by Instructional Fair • TS Denison
an imprint of

McGraw-Hill Children's Publishing

About the Author

Hal Torrance has worked for over a decade in teaching, both in middle school and at the elementary level. Social studies, language arts, and mathematics represent his areas of specialization. Hal has a teaching certificate from the state of Texas, and he has completed graduate work at both William & Mary and Texas A & M. Torrance and his family currently live in Virginia Beach, Virginia.

Credits

Author: Harold Torrance
Cover Design: Jeff Van Kanegan
Project Director/Editor: Jerry Aten
Editors: Mary Rose Hassinger, Alyson Kieda, Angella Phebus
Graphic Layout: Jannette M. Bole, C.J. Designs, Kruse Graphic Design

McGraw-Hill
Children's Publishing
A Division of The McGraw-Hill Companies

Published by Instructional Fair • TS Denison
An imprint of McGraw-Hill Children's Publishing
Copyright © 2002 McGraw-Hill Children's Publishing

Send all inquiries to:
McGraw-Hill Children's Publishing
3195 Wilson Drive NW
Grand Rapids, Michigan 49544

All Rights Reserved • Printed in the United States of America

Standards-Based Math—grades 7-8
ISBN: 0-7424-0217-7

1 2 3 4 5 6 7 8 9 07 06 05 04 03 02

Introduction to Teachers

Standards-Based Math for grades 7 and 8 was researched and written entirely with regard to current recommended National Council of Teachers of Mathematics (NCTM) standards. These standards serve as a framework or skeleton for the activities in this book. The ten proposed NCTM standards, which are a description of what an existing curriculum should enable students to know and do, are divided into two categories. The Content standards state the skill areas that students should learn. These are Number and Operations, Algebra, Geometry, Measurement, and Data Analysis and Probability. The Process standards, which guide instructors in planning lessons that enable students to acquire knowledge and achieve success, are the second set of standards. These are Problem Solving, Reasoning and Proof, Communication, Connections, and Representation.

For the purpose of this book, the Content standards have been highlighted, and each page is labeled with its appropriate standard and skill. The Process standards are naturally woven into the exercises on each page.

The following are simplified descriptions of the Content standards and examples of expectations.

Number and Operations
1. Understands numbers, number representations, relationships, and number systems
   • works easily with decimals, fractions, multiples, and integers
2. Understands basic operations and their relatedness
   • comfortably uses the distributive, commutative, and associative properties
3. Has computation and estimation fluency
   • selects and uses appropriate methods of computing and estimating

Algebra
1. Has full comprehension of relations, functions, and patterns in numbers
   • use tools such as graphs, tables, and symbolic rules to show a variety of patterns
2. Uses algebraic symbols
   • uses symbolic algebra to represent mathematical problems and to problem solve
3. Represents and shows quantitative relationships using models
4. Recognizes and evaluates change

Geometry

1. Has knowledge of two- and three-dimensional objects
   - classifies, describes, and understands the relationships using the objects' defining properties
2. Uses coordinate geometry
   - familiar with polygons
3. Recognizes symmetry and transformation
   - uses flips, turns, slides, and scaling to describe orientation of shapes
4. Solves problems using geometry

Measurement

1. Understands the processes of measurement
   - uses both metric and customary measurement
2. Uses a variety of methods to determine and show measurement
   - applies techniques to determine measurements such as circumference, length, area, volume

Data Analysis and Probability

1. Understands the need for and able to find and use data appropriately
   - designs questions and uses graphics to represent data
2. Utilizes statistics to answer questions
3. Makes inferences and predictions based upon data
4. Comprehends the basic principles of probability

Standards-Based Math has been divided into six major sections with the sequential nature of mathematics in mind. Most of the one- and two-page activities are self-contained and can be used independently. Each section begins with background material and a research activity pertaining to that section's theme.

Activities in this book involve students in the following:

- writing to convey math concepts and ideas

- developing a symbolic number system

- breaking the hidden code in a number pattern

- determining a financial pyramid scheme

- keeping a journal to evaluate a mathematical premise

- analyzing statistical information to determine its validity

- finding out why prime numbers are elusive and mysterious

- applying mathematical knowledge in a broad range of contexts

- coloring maps to determine whether a famous theorem actually works

- looking at geometric figures from new perspectives

- discovering that ancient peoples did have a knowledge of mathematics

- analyzing why credit card spending is better for the lenders than for the cardholder

- evaluating a stock investment against the interest paid on a bank account

- researching the math discoveries of non-Mediterranean/European cultures

- calculating mailing costs and deciding if the cost of the insurance is worth the money

- considering uses of data and learning techniques for working with data

- determining if an event is truly random

Standards-Based Math is arithmetic-based. Many seventh and eighth grade students are proficient in working problems requiring basic mathematical operations and procedures. Nonetheless, there are some students who still need additional review and practice to enable them to grasp the math concepts that have been deemed important for their particular grade level. Algebra topics are a part of this book and are given appropriate weight based on NCTM standards for this grade level. However, this book is not algebra based. It is rather a book filled with ideas and activities that will help seventh and eighth grade students to better master the variety of concepts and practices appropriate for this grade level.

Table of Contents

Table of Contents (cont.)

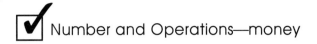

Money Matters

Since the dawn of time humans, have provided for their needs. These needs were once met by the practice of hunting and gathering. Eventually humans began settling areas and came to rely more on agriculture for their needs. Trade began to develop among these ancient communities as necessary commodities were bartered. Once money was developed, it provided a medium of exchange when trade goods were not available for barter. And even before there was money, there was mathematics.

Leonardo of Pisa, also known as Fibonacci, published *LiberAbaci* (*Book of the Abacus*) in 1202. This book was important not only for its content but also because it incorporated the Hindu-Arabic way of writing numerals that remains in use today. By the 1500s, the Arabic style of denoting numerals had all but replaced the use of Roman numerals in Europe, especially among the merchant classes for whom a knowledge of mathematics was essential for commerce.

Fibonacci's book would have represented an important primer for the merchant of the time. It provided a consistent mathematical method for dealing with currencies and conversions imposed by different systems of weighing and measuring goods. *LiberAbaci* represented, not a lofty mathematics text on astronomy or geometric proofs, but a method for solving the practical mathematics of commerce in everyday life.

The activities in this section are focused on the theme of financial and consumer math. It is rigorously based on the arithmetic of increase, especially in regard to using percentages to compute transactions involving taxes and interest. A connection between the understanding of mathematics and the ability to critically evaluate monetary transactions and consumer decisions will be established in this section.

For Further Research

Investigate some of the different cultures of the past such as the Babylonians, Romans, Chinese, Maya, or another group. Find out what system of mathematics they developed and used. Was it based on commerce or on other applications such as architecture or astronomy? How much of the knowledge they developed is applicable today, and what portions of it may have been passed to or used by later cultures? Write a short paper or prepare an oral report to summarize your findings.

Name _____

Percentages

The term **percentage** is used for denoting a particular part or a portion of some amount. Mathematical percentages describe precise amounts.

Working with a percentage requires understanding that it is a part of the whole. For example, 1% of some quantity is the same as saying $\frac{1}{100}$ of that quantity. From this example it is easy to see that percentages may be converted into decimal numbers.

Example:

20% equals **0.20** in decimal form.

When the percentage is dropped, the decimal place is moved 2 places to the left.

Likewise:

3%	equals	**0.03** in decimal form
.5%	equals	**0.005** in decimal form
300%	equals	**3.00** in decimal form
28.75%	equals	**0.2875** in decimal form

Most calculators have a % key which will quickly convert a percentage to its decimal number equivalent.

In the first blank, write the decimal equivalent of the percentage stated in the problem. Then solve the problem, using the second blank for your answer.

	Decimal Equivalent	Answer
Ex. 4% of 100	**0.04**	**4**
1. 98% of 500	.98	490
2. 80% of 5	.80	4
3. 6.5% of 12,000	.065	780
4. 0.8% of 120	.008	.96
5. 1% of 24	.01	.24
6. 150% of 30	1.5	45
7. 2.2% of 48	.022	1.856
8. 75% of 25,000	.75	18750
9. 8.6% of 16.25	.086	1.3975
10. 12% of 2.10	.12	.252

Percentages (cont.)

To convert a fraction to a percentage, follow this procedure:
A **fraction** *converts to a* **decimal number** which *converts to a* **percentage.**

$\frac{3}{4}$ = 3 divided by 4 = .75 = 75%

The decimal moves two places to the right when becoming a percentage from a decimal number.

Likewise:

$\frac{2}{12}$	=	2 ÷ 12	=	0.1666	=	**16.66%**
$\frac{4}{3}$	=	4 ÷ 3	=	1.333	=	**133.33%**
$\frac{1}{100}$	=	1 ÷ 100	=	0.01	=	**1%**
$\frac{375}{10000}$	=	375 ÷ 10000	=	0.0375	=	**3.75%**
$3\frac{1}{2}$	=	3 + (1 ÷ 2)	=	3.50	=	**350%**

Fill in the missing information in the conversions below.

	Fraction	**=**	**Decimal**	**=**	**Percentage**
Ex.	$\frac{3}{8}$		**0.375**		**37.5 %**
1.	$\frac{1}{7}$		.1429		14.29%
2.	$\frac{4}{5}$		.8		80%
3.	$2\frac{5}{8}$		2.625		262.5
4.	$\frac{2}{4}$		0.50		50%
5.	$\frac{3}{4}$		0.75		75%
6.	$\frac{1}{5}$		0.20		20%
7.	$\frac{5}{5}$		1.00		100%
8.	$\frac{9}{10}$		.90		90%
9.	$\frac{3}{5}$		.60		60%
10.			.6667		66.67 %
11.	$\frac{22}{99}$		.2222		22.22%
12.	$\frac{34}{8}$		4.25		425%

$x = .6666$
$10x = 6.6666$
$9x = 6$
$x = \frac{6}{99}$

Name _____

Sales Tax

A sales tax is a fee assessed on the value of goods or services sold.
A sales tax is an example of a percentage being used for computing part of a financial transaction. Here is how sales tax is computed.

Tax Rate x Price of Item = Sales Tax

Example: Carla is planning to buy a large screen television. The retail price of the television is $1,225. The tax rate where she lives is 5%. What will the sales tax be on this purchase?

Tax Rate x Price of Item = Sales Tax

The percentage tax rate should first be converted to a decimal number.
$$0.05 \times \$1225 = \text{Sales Tax}$$
$$\$61.25 = \text{Sales Tax}$$

For each of the purchases listed below, compute the sales tax. The tax rate as a percentage is listed in parentheses.

1. $380.00   (8.8%) $33.44
2. $4.25   (4.5%) $0.19
3. $12,000   (1.25%) $150
4. $69.99   (3.4%) $2.38
5. $120.75   (6.66%) $8.04
6. $0.88   (5%) $0.04
7. $100,000   (0.05%) $50
8. $55,000   (7.5%) $4125
9. $8.50   (9%) $0.77
10. $22.99   (3.25%) $0.75

Short Answer

11. In general, what effect do you think a high sales tax rate has on sales of consumer items? I think they won't be sold as much as a low sales tax.

Sales Tax (cont.)

Short Answer (cont.)

12. What are the financial implications for a state with a high sales tax rate that borders a state with no sales tax? *People may want to buy things from their bordering state than from their own.*

13. Many state sales tax rates are around 5%. Describe a method that consumers could use for making a quick mental estimate of the sales tax on a given purchase. *You can find 5% quickly by finding 10% of the item, then find half of that.*

Problem Solving

14. George is buying a new computer. A system he likes is priced at $1,099. If the sales tax rate is 4.25%, how much sales tax would be owed on this purchase?

    __$46.77__

    1099
    x.0425
    5495 0767 5
    21980
    43960 0
    46.7675
    + 0000
    46.7675

15. Marcie is buying business equipment, which will cost $2,700. If the sales tax rate is 5%, what will her total cost be for the equipment?

    __$2835__

    2700
    x .05
    13500
    00000
    135.00

    2700
    135
    2 635

16. The local newsstand must collect a sales tax of 2% on printed materials and a sales tax of 4% on all other goods. What total sales tax will a customer owe if buying a magazine for $4.95 and a box of candy for $0.80?

    ___.04___

    4.95
    .02
    990
    0000
    .0990

    .01
    .03
    .04

    .80
    x.04
    320
    000
    0320

17. Sarah was charged $1.80 sales tax on a purchase of $16.40. If the sales tax rate is 4.5%, how much was she overcharged in sales tax?

    __1.05__

    16.40
    .045
    8200
    6 600
    2 6 5 600
    12.73800

    1.80
    - .75
    1.05

Commissions

A **commission** is a percentage-based compensation, ordinarily paid to a person who is involved in the sale of some product. Typically, sales personnel will earn a commission for items they are able to sell for a business.

Here is how basic commission is computed:

Commission Rate x Price of Item = Commission Earned

Example: Sylvia is a real estate agent. She receives a 2.5% commission on the sale of houses. How much would her commission be on the sale of a $234,000 house? (The percentage commission rate should first be converted to a decimal number.

$$0.025 \times \$234,000 = \text{Commission Earned}$$
$$\$5,850 = \text{Commission Earned}$$

Compute the commission for each of the situations below.

1. A 1% commission paid by an electronics store to the employee who sold a camera costing $589.00.
   $.06

2. A 6% commission paid to a real estate broker on the sale of a $335,000 house.
   $20,100

3. Brenda is paid a 2% commission on the first month's rent of $740.00 for referring anyone who signs an apartment lease.
   $14.80

4. John is given a $\frac{1}{4}$% commission for advising a client on the closing of a deal worth $1,200,000.
   $3000

Name _____

Commissions (cont.)

Solve the problems involving commission situations.

5. Roland earns a 24% commission for each $499.00 vacuum cleaner he is able to sell on his door-to-door sales route.

   <u>119.76</u>

6. Martin is paid a commission rate of 11.75% for the sale of livestock and a commission rate of 3.5% for hay and grain sold. How much money will Martin earn in commissions during a month in which he sells $15,600 in livestock and $20,340 in hay/grain sales?

   <u>2544.90</u>

   $$1833.00$$
   $$+ \ 711.90$$
   $$2544.90$$

7. Sally is considering a sales job. She currently earns a fixed salary of $18,200 per year. The sales job she is considering offers no fixed salary, but an 8% commission rate on sales made by employees. Sally was told that the top salesperson at this company closed $320,000 in sales the previous year. How much more did the top salesperson earn than Sally?

   <u>$64000</u>

   $$\begin{array}{r} 320000 \\ - \ 256000 \\ \hline 64000 \end{array}$$

   $$\begin{array}{r} 320000 \\ \times \quad .08 \\ \hline 2560000 \\ 0000000 \\ \hline 25600.00 \end{array}$$

8. Mallorie took a fifteen-minute break from her sales job at a computer store. The cash register clerk who filled in for her sold a $2,610 computer system, thus earning the commission for that sale. How much money did Mallorie lose while on break if her commission rate is 1.75%, considering that the computer sale would ordinarily have been hers?

   <u>$45.68</u>

   $$\begin{array}{r} 2610 \\ \times .0175 \\ \hline 13050 \\ 182700 \\ 261000 \\ 00000 \end{array}$$

   45.6750

Short Answer

9. Why do you think a salesperson might try harder to complete sales if the base salary is small, but their commission rate is high? They would do this because if they sell more products they could gain more money.

10. Instead of paying their employees commissions on sales, why would some businesses rather pay them a salary based on how well they work with customers or on how well the business is doing overall? If they have a very good sale they may not want to give them to much money.

14 IF87128 Standards-Based Math

Building a Pyramid the Old-Fashioned Way

Financial schemes began not long after the use of money. The success of most con games relies on the greed factor of those involved. Every year, countless people are tricked out of their money because they believe it is possible to make a large return on their investment.

History is full of stories of financial fraud. During the 1600s in Holland, the price of tulip bulbs began to rise rapidly. Swindlers and opportunists took advantage of the tulip market and cheated thousands with overpriced tulip bulbs. People were lured by the chance of making easy money, since it looked as if prices were going to continue to rise. The strategy was to buy a few bulbs and sell them the next week once the price had risen. Eventually the tulip bulb prices became so high that some who had invested could not get their money back before the prices crashed.

A similar episode occurred in America in the 1920s. Charles Ponzi introduced a scheme where people invested in postal reply coupons that could be redeemed in other countries for postage. Ponzi took in nearly $10 million, a staggering sum for the 1920s, by convincing people that money could be made on the exchange rates involved in redeeming the postal coupons. People invested with few questioning how postal transactions involving only pennies could generate such immense profits. The scheme collapsed cheating thousands out of their investments.

Example: Here is how one variation of a pyramid scheme works. Mr. Golden tells six acquaintances to each give him $10.00 as an investment. He may return part or all of this money later as profit to instill confidence in investors. Eventually, Mr. Golden will collect the money of these investors and will ask them each to find more investors to contribute. Some pyramid schemes allow those recruiting new members to keep a portion of the monies collected to create enthusiasm for recruiting more members. As the money flows from the bottom of the pyramid toward the top, the amount of money and new members needed to sustain the pyramid becomes mathematically unsustainable and the pyramid collapses.

Pyramid schemes are characterized by the need for new members to sustain the money inflow and by the fact that there is usually no true underlying investment.

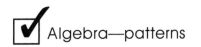

Name _____

Building a Pyramid the Old-Fashioned Way (cont.)

Answer the questions below involving pyramid schemes. Draw a diagram to help with the calculations.

1. Bert sent a letter to 20 people asking them to each send him $50.00 to support an innovative computer idea he is developing. (Bert's idea is to have other people pay for his next new computer.)

   A. If 14 of the 20 people respond by sending Bert the $50.00, how much money has he collected at this point? $700

   B. Bert mailed another letter to the 14 people who had already sent him money. He asked each of them to find 6 new investors. Bert told the 14 original investors to collect $50.00 from each new investor, keep $20.00 from each new investor, and forward the rest of the money to him. If Bert's request is met, how much money will he receive from this new wave of investors? $420

   C. Bert has notified the newest level of investors, giving them the same instructions as he gave to the original 14. However, he told them to keep only $10.00 for themselves, give $10.00 to the person who recruited them, and send the rest to him. How much will Bert receive from this newest level of investors?
   $280

   D. When the police arrest Bert (since pyramid schemes are considered fraud and are illegal), how much money will they contend that Bert's pyramid generated in total? $1300

Interest

Interest is the amount of money banks pay you for using your money while it is on deposit. Simple interest is the percentage rate paid for this money over a determined period of time, typically expressed in terms of a one-year period. Banks pay you for depositing money because they are allowed to loan out a portion of overall deposits at higher interest rates, thereby making a profit. This is how banking fundamentally works as a business.

Here is how simple interest is computed:

Interest Rate x Amount of Money on Deposit = Simple Interest Earned
(also called principal)

Example 1: Charles placed $1,000 into a savings account, which pays $4\frac{3}{4}$% interest per year. How much interest will this account earn after one year has passed? Remember to convert the percentage rate into a decimal number before beginning the actual computation.

Interest Rate x Amount of Money on Deposit = Simple Interest Earned
   0.0475   x $1000   = Simple Interest Earned
            $47.50   = Simple Interest Earned

Example 2: Simple interest works the same way when applied to loans. Charlotte borrowed $88,600 in the form of a construction loan to build a house. The loan has an interest rate of 9.25% and is due at the end of one year. How much money will Charlotte owe the bank when the loan is due?

Interest Rate x Amount of Money Borrowed = Simple Interest Owed
   0.0925   x $88,600   = Simple Interest Owed
           $8195.50   = Simple Interest Owed

The amount that Charlotte owes the bank is her loan principal plus the simple interest owed.

$$\$88,600 + \$8195.50 = \$96,795.50$$

Charlotte will owe the bank a total of $96,795.50 at the end of her loan term.

Interest (cont.)

Read each of the questions below about interest on deposits and loans. Determine what the question is asking, then make the necessary computations to determine an answer.

1. Jorge bought a certificate of deposit at a bank for $10,000. He agreed to leave his money with the bank for one year at an interest rate of $7\frac{1}{2}$%. How much money will Jorge earn in interest on his deposit of $10,000?

    $6750

    10,000
    × .075
    50000
    7000 00
    750 0 0 00   6750000

2. Lucinda is considering the purchase of a new computer at a cost of $880.00. She has the money in her savings account, which is currently earning 5.5% interest per year. If she waits one year before buying the new computer, how much interest will she be able to collect on her money?

    $48.40

    880
    × .055
    4400   484 00
    440 0 0
    000 0 0

3. Rita took out a $2,000 loan, using her car as collateral. The loan was made through a finance company, at an interest rate of 23.99% per year. How much interest will Rita owe if it is not repaid before the year ends?

    $2479.80

    2,000

4. Harvey owns a local business. He arranged a one-month loan with his bank in order to stock extra inventory for a special sale he is advertising. Harvey borrowed $20,000 at $1\frac{1}{2}$% interest for this one-month period. How much money will Harvey need to repay the bank at the end of the month?

    $20,300

5. Angie has $12,200 in a savings account that pays 8% interest per year. She knows she will need $13,000 in exactly one year to meet her daughter's tuition payment. Will there be enough money in this account in a year's time to meet this obligation?

    yes

    12,200
    976
    13176

Credit Card Buying

A credit card is like a bank loan but allows the consumer to make immediate purchases. Most credit card companies charge a yearly fee for issuing the card, and then charge a yearly rate of interest for balances left on the card. The yearly interest rate is ordinarily assessed as monthly interest against the outstanding loan balance.

Example: Carmen's credit card carries a yearly interest rate of 18%. Since there are 12 months in a year, Carmen is effectively charged 1.5% interest per month on her outstanding balance. If Carmen has a current balance on her credit card of $624.88 and makes no other purchases or payments, how much will this balance cost her in interest after another month has passed?

Recall the simple interest formula from a previous section

Interest Rate	x	Amount of Money Borrowed	=	Interest Owed
0.015	x	$624.88	=	Interest Owed
	$9.37		=	Interest Owed

In general, credit card debt is a costly way of borrowing money. In this example, if Carmen were to make no payment the next month, the interest owed would become part of the loan balance and interest would be assessed on that portion of the loan balance as well. This is an example of compounding interest. Keep in mind that many credit card issuers might require that Carmen only make a monthly payment of $20.00. It will take longer to repay the loan because much of the minimum payment is being used to pay interest.

Answer the questions below involving credit card purchases.

1. Susan has a credit card with a yearly fee of $35.00. She seldom uses this card and always pays the balance in full to avoid owing interest. In January, the credit card issuer sent her a bill for the yearly fee of $35.00. Susan forgot to pay this bill. The following month, she still owed the $35.00 plus the $1\frac{3}{4}$% monthly interest charge on that balance. How much will Susan need to send to pay her outstanding balance completely?

_____

2. A department store sales clerk sold John a bedroom suite for $1,800. The sales clerk

Credit Card Buying (cont.)

also talked John into signing up for their department store credit card, saying it was "a great deal since there was no payment due for a month." Upon receiving his bill a month later, John was surprised to find that a $15.00 fee had been charged for opening his credit card account and that a 1.5% interest rate had been applied to the entire outstanding balance for the month. Suddenly, John realized that "no payment due for a month" did not mean that no interest was due for a month. How much does he now owe on his department store credit card account?

_____

3. Bonnie took a vacation and charged everything on her credit card. When her credit card bill came it was for $8,588. She paid $1,000 toward the balance due, knowing that the rest of the balance would have interest charged against it. If her credit card's monthly interest rate is $1\frac{1}{4}$% on outstanding balances, how much will she owe on this credit card account when next month's bill arrives? Bonnie plans to make no new purchases or payments during that time period.

_____

Solving by Estimation

4. Sheila vowed not to use her credit card again. She had been making only the minimum payments each month and was making very little headway against the actual debt owed. If her monthly interest bill is nearly $50.00 and the annual interest rate on this card is 15%, about how much is her balance? _____

5. Miguel bought a $1,200 guitar with his credit card. It is the only charge he has made to the card. He figures that paying $100.00 on his credit card per month will pay off the entire balance in about 13 months. What is the approximate annual interest rate on Miguel's credit card?

_____

Currency Exchange

Each country has its own form of currency. How do these currencies relate to each other in a mathematical sense? How is one currency exchanged for another?

Currencies of the world are bought and sold in large amounts, just as company stocks are sold on the stock market or as livestock is sold at an auction. These currency transactions set the value of one currency against another in a mathematical relationship.

The exchange rates for many of the world's currencies may be found by looking in a newspaper or by checking a financial site online. Often they are listed in tables that show a currency such as the Euro and a list of other currencies based on the value of the Euro. Depending on the currency, it may take several of a particular unit to purchase a single Euro. For example, at this writing it takes over six French francs to buy a single Euro, but a single Euro is not enough to purchase a British pound.

For Further Research

Find a current listing of currency exchange rates and complete the following:

1. 50 U.S. Dollars   =   _____ Australian Dollars
2. 40 French Francs   =   _____ Japanese Yen
3. 210 British Pounds   =   _____ U.S. Dollars
4. 38 Swiss Francs   =   _____ French Francs
5. 80,00 Japanese Yen   =   _____ U.S. Dollars
6. 40 German Marks   =   _____ French Francs
7. 1000 French Francs   =   _____ British Pounds
8. 50 German Marks   =   _____ Australian Dollars
9. 12 U.S. Dollars   =   _____ Swiss Francs

For each of the transactions above, compute the equivalent number of Euros.

Name _____

Auctions

Auction houses most often work on a commission basis. A seller places something, such as an expensive vase, with an auction house. The auction house may charge a flat fee (a listing fee) for accepting the vase and including it in an upcoming sale. It is agreed that if the item is sold, the auction house will also collect a commission, usually about 10% of the selling price. Some auction houses impose a buyer's commission as well, but this is not as common since the practice may discourage people from bidding.

Auction Commission Rate x Selling Price of Item = Commission Earned

Example: Mr. Smith has placed an expensive painting with Lloyd Street Auction Company to be sold to the highest bidder. He's agreed that from the "hammer price" (the price at which the bidding stops), he will pay the auction house a 12% commission and a flat $200.00 listing fee. How much will Mr. Smith owe the auction house if his painting sells for $4,250? (Remember: the percentage rate must first be converted to decimal form.)

Auction Commission Rate x Selling Price of Item = Commission Earned
        0.12   x $4,250   = Commission Earned
             $510.00   = Commission Earned

Mr. Smith will owe the auction house $510.00 commission, plus the $200.00 listing fee, for a total of $710.00. These fees usually are deducted from the amount due the seller once all accounts have been settled at the close of the auction.

Solve each of the problems below. Some may involve more work than simply computing an auction commission.

1. Trixie consigned an antique dresser to be sold at auction. There was no listing fee, but an 18% commission was charged on the sale price of the dresser. The dresser sold for $720.00. How much money will she receive from the sale after the commission is paid?

_____

Auctions (cont.)

2. Estelle bought a set of dishes at an auction for $240.00. She had not read the "fine print" on her bidder's card, so when she went to pay for the dishes she found out that she owed a 5% buyer's commission as well as a 6.5% sales tax on the price of the dishes. What was the total cost of the dishes?

_____

3. Barton wants to sell his coin collection. He thinks the collection will sell for $25,000 at auction, but he is put off by the 15% commission rate charged by Golden Hammer Auction House. In comparison, Heavy Gavel Auction House charges a listing fee of $500.00 and a commission rate of only 12%. If the coins bring what Barton thinks they will, and each house is equally capable of selling the coins, with which firm should Barton go?

_____

4. Ernie is selling his baseball card collection by using an online auction company. This particular company charges only $1.50 to list an item and 2.5% of the final bid price as a commission once the auction is completed. How much will Ernie be left with from the sale of a $12.00 baseball card once these fees are paid?

_____

5. Gregory bought a lamp at a yard sale for $45.00, thinking it was a vintage art deco period piece. Gregory paid a $2.00 listing fee with a local auction house to sell the lamp for him. The auction house also charges a hefty commission of 20% on all items sold. The lamp brought only $12.50 when it was auctioned. How much money did Gregory lose on this lamp investment?

_____

Short Answer

6. If you are a seller and believe your item will bring a lot more than is expected at auction, why would it be in your best interest to negotiate a flat fee that is slightly higher than normal and a commission rate that is much less than normal?

Stocks

Stated simply, a share of **stock** is a small piece of ownership in a company. A large company will typically have millions of shares of stock outstanding. These shares of stock are bought and sold each day on the world's various stock exchanges. These exchanges are similar to an auction, where stock prices are determined by factors such as a company's profitability, its future outlook, and how much people are willing to pay for a share.

Investors may buy some stocks directly from a company, but most often stocks are bought through a broker. A broker earns a commission for buying or selling stock on behalf of an investor. Typically the commission is a flat fee, instead of a percentage.

Historically, stock prices were listed as dollar amounts with fractional portions when applicable. In recent years, exchanges have changed to quoting stock prices in decimals, making the precise amounts easier to determine at a glance.

In general, an investor's cost basis on a stock purchase is found in the following way.

(Individual Share Price x Number of Shares Purchased) + Commission = Cost Basis

Example 1: Brooke placed an order to buy 1,200 shares of stock in a company at a price of $41.25 per share. Her broker charged her a commission of $175.00 for this transaction. What was her total cost basis for these shares of stock?

$$(1{,}200 \ \times \ \$41.25) \ + \ \$175.00 \ = \ \text{Cost Basis}$$
$$\$49{,}500 \qquad + \ \$175.00 \ = \ \text{Cost Basis}$$
$$\$49{,}675 \ = \ \text{Cost Basis}$$

Brooke's cost basis in these shares was $49,675 for the lot, or about $41.39 per share. The per share figure was derived by dividing the cost basis by the total number of shares purchased.

Stocks (cont.)

Example 2: An investor bought 100 shares of stock in a new health research company, paying $3.75 per share. The commission paid on this purchase was $35.00. What was the investor's cost basis for this stock purchase?

$$(100 \times \$3.75) \quad + \quad \$35.00 \quad = \quad \text{Cost Basis}$$
$$\$375.00 \quad + \quad \$35.00 \quad = \quad \text{Cost Basis}$$
$$\$405.00 \quad\quad\quad\quad = \quad \text{Cost Basis}$$

The investor's cost basis in these shares was $405.00 for the lot, or $4.05 per share.

In the problems below, compute the cost basis for the situations described.

1. Denise bought 160 shares of stock in a paper products manufacturing company at a cost of $24.40 per share. She paid no commission for this purchase since the company sold her the stock directly. What was her cost basis for this lot?

   _____

2. Alfred got a hot tip on an oil company stock and bought 200 shares in the company at a cost of $88.88, paying a commission on this trade of $75.00. What is his cost basis on this lot of stock?

   _____

3. An investor bought 200 shares of stock in a company at $6.75 per share. Later in the day, the investor bought another 100 shares in this same company, this time at $7.25 each. The investor paid a commission of $24.95 on each purchase. What is this investor's total cost basis for the 300 shares?

   _____

4. A broker called one of his clients and suggested he buy 300 shares of stock in an athletic shoe manufacturer at a cost of $45.50 per share. The customer thought about it a few moments, then agreed to buy 125 shares. The price of the stock had dropped to $44.12 once the order was put through. Commission on this purchase was $69.00. What is the client's cost basis per share in this stock?

   _____

Stock Sales

Selling a stock works much the same way as buying a stock. Typically, an order is placed with a broker to sell the stock, and a commission is paid on the transaction. **Total proceeds** is a term often used for describing the total sale price of a stock lot. The profit made on a stock sale is that amount above the cost of the stock. In cases where the cost basis is larger than total proceeds, a loss has occurred.

Total Proceeds	**– Total Cost Basis**	**= Profit**
	(includes all commissions plus original cost of stock)	(or loss if this figure is negative)

Example: Jane's original cost basis for 100 shares of a publishing company was $3,886.58. When she sold these shares, total proceeds on the sale were $4,230. The broker charged a commission of $45 on the sale of this stock. How much profit did she make on the sale of this stock?

$4,230   – ($3,886.58 + $45.00)   =   Profit
$4,230   – $3,931.58   =   Profit
         $298.42   =   Profit

Jane turned a profit of $298.42 on this sale of stock.

For each of the situations below involving stock transactions, determine the profit, the loss, or the average cost per share as specified.

1. Timothy has 235 shares of stock in a retail book company for which he paid a total of $2,010.50. When he sold the stock, it brought $12.25 per share, and Timothy paid a commission of $28.00 on the sale. How much profit did he make on the sale of this stock? _____

2. Russell discovered the Maui Nut, Mango, and Coffee Farm while on vacation. He called his broker and authorized the purchase of 2,000 shares of this company's stock. The shares were purchased at a cost of $18.75 each, and Russell paid a commission of $300.00 on the purchase. A few months later, Russell authorized his broker to sell all of his shares in this company. Since other investors were also selling stocks, the shares brought only $15.25 each, and Russell paid another $300.00 commission on the sale. How much money did Russell lose on this investment?

Stock Sales (cont.)

3. Trisha bought 75 shares of stock in an entertainment company for a total cost of $1,626.65. She paid a commission of $75.00 when she sold this stock. The shares brought a very good price, $44.25 per share. How much profit did Trisha make on the entertainment company stock?

_____

4. Neal invested $4,500.75 to buy 18,000 shares of a company doing research in artificial intelligence. A friend from work recommended the company, and Neal was impressed by the fact that the friend had already purchased 30,000 shares of stock in this company for himself. The stock turned out to be a good investment for Neal. He later sold 6,000 of his shares at $8.12 per share, paying a commission of $225.00 on the sale. Neal is keeping the other 12,000 shares of stock in this company. How much profit has he already made on this stock?

_____

5. An investor bought a block of 300 shares of stock, paying a total of $5,808.55 for the shares, including commission. What is the investor's average cost per share for this stock?

_____

6. A mutual fund manager paid $48.44 per share for a block of 20,000 shares of stock. The purchase was made through another branch of the same investment company and the commission for acquiring the shares is not part of the mutual fund manager's cost basis for the stock. The next day, the price of this stock dropped to $44.75 per share, and the mutual fund manager bought another 5,000 shares of the same stock to "round out his position." Once again, the purchase was made through another department of the company and no commission was assessed. What is the average cost per share of the 25,000 shares?

_____

Name _____

More Work with Financial Math

Solve the problems below.

1. Walter is going to use money from his savings account to buy a new car. He has $26,200 in his account. Where Walter lives, sales tax on this kind of purchase is $4\frac{1}{4}\%$. If the car he is planning to buy costs $24,244.33 before the sales tax is added, how much money will Walter have left in his account after buying the car and paying the sales tax?

_____

2. Last year, Stewart was paid a base salary of $12,000 per year and a commission of 3% on the total dollar value of sales he closed. He sold $1,120,000 worth of company products. This year, his boss announced that Stewart's new commission rate will be cut to 2.8% on sales, but his base salary will be raised to $14,000 per year. This has given Stewart cause for concern. How much less money would Stewart have made last year if this plan had been in place then?

_____

3. A painting by a famous Impressionist sold through an auction house by private treaty, meaning that the sales price was not publicly disclosed. This particular auction house works on a commission rate of 10%. If it is discovered that the commission on this painting was $400,000, what was the sale price of the painting?

_____

Short Answer
4. Banks accept money into savings accounts, then loan the money out, charging interest for such loans. How is this different from a pyramid scheme?

Name _____

Number Patterns

Prior to the Spanish invasion of Central America in the early 1500s, the Mayan civilization worked extensively with mathematics. Much of Mayan mathematics related to astronomy. The Mayans developed several different calendars based on varying lengths for a year. These calendars were built around religious observations or government functions. One of their calendars was remarkably similar to our own and had a 365-day year. Another calendar employed a cycle of 819 days.

Mayan carvings found on the sides of stone pillars resemble what is referred to today as the dot-and-dash numbering system. A dot denoted one, a dash denoted five, and another shell-like symbol stood for zero. Their number system was loosely based on 20. Interestingly, the carvings were constructed every 20 years and included inscriptions detailing noteworthy events of the previous 20 years.

The ancient Egyptian's were probably the first to divide the calendar day into 24 units. Their calendar was also largely based on predictable astrological observations. Of special importance to the Egyptians was tracking the rising of the star Sirius, as it roughly coincided with the flooding of the Nile. The Egyptian's agricultural system was based on this yearly flooding of the Nile.

A number of ancient cultures perceived the passing of time as a basic mathematical pattern. Looking back, it can be seen that astrological observations were one of the most commonly occurring mathematical expressions of these cultures.

The activities in this section are built around the theme of patterns and their place in mathematics. Special emphasis is placed on developing the skills needed to investigate mathematical patterns. This involves being able to recognize a pattern and then learn how to identify the factor(s) that make a pattern work. Being able to identify and define a pattern is not only a mathematics application but is also the basis for research in a number of areas including the sciences and business.

For Further Research
Choose an ancient culture and study its calendar. Take notes and organize your thoughts into a short paper or use to present an oral report. What was the basis for the calendar? Was it astrologically based or tied to some other system? What other observations can you make concerning the culture's calendar? You might want to consider the reasons behind the calendar and the need for tracking certain yearly events.

Name _____

Patterns

A mathematical pattern is characterized by items that appear in a set order based on a rule or condition being met. The number series 1, 2, 3, 4, 5, 6, 7, 8,... is a simple number pattern. In this number pattern, each digit is one larger than the preceding digit. This simple number pattern increases at a rate of +1 per interval and could be described algebraically by the expression $n + 1$.

In general, a number pattern that is increasing at a steady rate will be based on addition, while a number pattern that is decreasing at a steady rate will be based on subtraction. Likewise, a number pattern that is increasing rapidly will be based on multiplication, while a number pattern decreasing rapidly will be based on division.

Example 1: Find the missing member of the following number pattern.

168, 154, 140, _____ , 112, 98, 84

Since this pattern seems to be decreasing steadily, it points to subtraction as the likely operation. An inspection of the intervals between numbers confirms a loss of 14 at each interval, or $y - 14$. The missing member of this pattern is 126.

Example 2: Sometimes a pattern may be acted upon by more than one operation. Look at the example below.

12, 24, 22, 44, _____ , 84, 82, 164

In general, the pattern is increasing rapidly but with small setbacks in the intermediate steps. Multiplication at one interval is followed by subtraction at the next interval: x 2, then – 2, or p x 2, $p - 2$ alternating. The missing member is 42.

Example 3: While the next pattern has no numbers, it follows the rules of order for the alphabet.

A, AA, AB, B, BB, BC, _____ , _____ , CD, D, DD, DE

In this pattern, the letter first appears singly, then it doubles. Next it combines with the following letter in the series. At this point, the new letter takes over and continues the series. The missing members are C, CC.

Name _____

Patterns (cont.)

Solve for the missing members of each series. Where applicable, describe the pattern algebraically.

1. 3, 8, 15, 20, _____ , 32, 39, _____ , 51, 56
   Pattern _____

2. 100, 120, 140, 160, 180, _____ , _____ , _____
   Pattern _____

3. 212, _____ , 134, 67, 95, 47.5
   Pattern _____

4. 3, 9, 81, _____ ,
   Pattern _____

5. 1, 5, 25, 125, _____ , _____
   Pattern _____

Solve problems 6–8, then write a short description of each pattern.

6. –6, –5, –3, 0, 4, _____ , _____ , _____

7. X, U, R, _____ , _____ , I

8. △△☐☐△△☐☐△△☐☐

More About Patterns

Perhaps the most famous pattern ever defined is that of Leonardo of Pisa. Also called Fibonacci, this mathematician's work became famous in the early 1200s. After observing the proliferation of rabbits, Fibonacci defined a pattern that has implications for much of the natural world. The pattern begins 1, 1, 2, 3, 5...

1. Beginning at the 2, each following number in the series is the sum of the two previous numbers. Try filling in the values for the blanks below.

   1, 1, 2, 3, 5, _____, _____, _____, _____, _____, 89, 144, _____, _____

   You can see that Fibonacci's pattern is based on addition and its members tend to rise gradually in size.

2. What if the series began with 3, 4, and maintained a pattern in which each of the two preceding members are added to form the next member? Try filling in the blanks for this variation of the Fibonacci sequence.

   3, 4, _____, _____, _____, _____, 47, 76, _____, _____

   Mathematicians have made observations about the ratios of numbers in the Fibonacci sequence, and the similarity of ratios in other series that employ the Fibonacci pattern. Look at the values 89 and 144 given in the Fibonacci sequence above.

   $\frac{89}{144} = 0.618055$ (carried only to 6 decimal places)

   Now look at the second series.

   $\frac{47}{76} = 0.618421$ (carried only to 6 decimal places)

Activity

Create your own variation of the Fibonacci sequence. Carry out your series to about 20 members. Try comparing the ratios of its members to those of the Fibonacci sequence. What observation can you make about the ratios you've found when compared to those of the original Fibonacci sequence?

Decimation

Decimation is the process of reducing an amount according to a set pattern. "Deci," meaning 10, literally refers to a one-tenth portion, although the term **decimation** can be used for indicating the reduction of other amounts. Look at the diagram below.

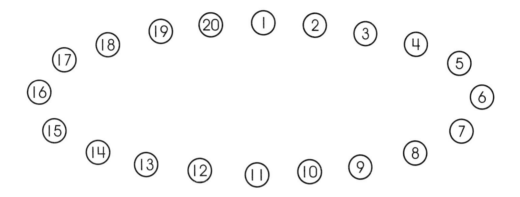

Assume that the above diagram represents personnel files stored in a data bank. A clerk has been asked to devise a system based on a criterion other than alphabetical order where employee files can be checked systematically for completeness. If the clerk begins with file number 1 and checks every third file, how many repetitions of this process would it take to complete the task of checking all records? If the clerk begins at file 1 and counts three places, the first file examined is file 3, the next is file 6, the next is file 9, and so forth. You can see from the example that all of the files would have been checked by the end of the third rotation of this pattern.

Answer the questions below involving decimation. Draw a diagram to help.

1. If 14 people have applied for a job, and the search committee is eliminating half of the candidates at each stage of the interview process, how many stages will get the candidate pool down to one person? Keep in mind that no more than half of the candidates may be eliminated at any single stage. _____

2. During a gasoline shortage some years ago, cars with even-numbered license plates could fill their tanks on certain days, and cars with odd-numbered license plates could fill on alternating days. How is this a decimation system?

_____

Functions

A simple algebraic function exists between two variables when there is a corresponding relationship between one variable and the value of the other.

Example: Is y a function of x in the following expression?

$$y = 4x$$

If values are inserted for x, it is easy to determine a corresponding value for y. For example, if I is inserted for the value of x, then y becomes 4.

$$y = 4(1)$$
$$y = 4$$

Another way to write this same function is in terms of only one variable.

$$f(x) = 4x$$

This way of writing a function uses $f(x)$ as a substitute for y. It means essentially the same thing. When a value for x is inserted in the expression, a corresponding $f(x)$ value is created.

For each of the functions, find the value of that function using the information given.

1. $y = 2x + 1$
   A. $y =$ _____ when x is 4.   B. $y =$ _____ when x is 7.

2. $y = x - 1$
   A. $y =$ _____ when x is 0.   B. $y =$ _____ when x is 3.

3. $f(x) = x/2$
   A. $f(x) =$ _____ when x is 4.   B. $f(x) =$ _____ when x is 1.

4. $f(p) = 3p$
   A. $f(p) =$ _____ when p is $\frac{1}{2}$.   B. $f(p) =$ _____ when p is –2.

5. $y = x^2$
   A. $y =$ _____ when x is 2.   B. $y =$ _____ when x is – 4.

Name _____

Summation

The symbol for the Greek letter sigma is a symbol sometimes used in mathematics. It represents the sum of a series of numbers. This is its basic formula.

$$\sum_{k=1}^{n} k = \frac{n(n+1)}{2}$$

Here is how the formula works. Let's say you need to know the sum of the numbers 1 through 10. Set up the values in the summation formula, then solve.

$$\sum_{k=1}^{10} k = \frac{10(10+1)}{2}$$

$$\sum_{k=1}^{10} k = \frac{10(11)}{2} = \frac{110}{2} = 55$$

Use the summation formula to find the sum of the following series.

1. $\displaystyle\sum_{k=1}^{16}$

2. $\displaystyle\sum_{k=1}^{24}$

3. $\displaystyle\sum_{k=1}^{100}$

4. $\displaystyle\sum_{k=1}^{31}$

5. $\displaystyle\sum_{k=1}^{1000}$

Name _____

Tessellations

Dutch artist Maurits Cornelis Escher (1898–1972) is probably best known for his work in tessellations. By the 1950s, Escher was already a prominent graphic artist, working mostly in Europe. But it was his forays into the world of geometric art that caught the attention of mathematicians and captivated the world of art. Escher's tessellation drawings, while quite advanced, are based on the simple premise of any tessellation. Tessellations are patterns of geometric figures that will perfectly adjoin to cover completely an area in a continuing pattern. This process is sometimes referred to as tiling.

Escher departed from using simple geometric figures for his tessellation drawings. By shifting bits of a figure and determining how figures might nest together, Escher was able to create complex tessellations. He employed a variety of themes with subjects such as fish, birds, salamanders, and even people riding horses.

Activity

Try experimenting with basic geometric shapes such as triangles, quadrilaterals, pentagons, hexagons, and octagons. Try to determine which kinds of figures will naturally tessellate and which require a complementary figure to complete a pattern. Once you have determined a method for tessellating figures, try producing a finished drawing to illustrate this concept.

Name _____

Parts and Wholes

Clay tablets dating back nearly 4,000 years show that the ancient Babylonians had a system of mathematics. They inscribed cuneiform symbols denoting a number system based on 60 on the clay tablets. Their base 60 system of mathematics is similar to our present-day method of keeping time.

Many thousands of these clay tablets still exist, bearing mathematics applications from business transactions to academic works. One Babylonian clay tablet is thought to portray examples of Pythagorean triangles over a thousand years before Pythagoras was born. Interestingly, after being used for mathematical applications, these clay tablets were sometimes reused as building materials.

The ancient Egyptians had a system of computing numbers based on a combination of doubling numerals and adding different combinations of multiples. The Egyptians computed fractions in a similar fashion, but their method was somewhat cumbersome and quite unlike the precise method we use today.

The activities in this section focus on the concept that numbers are composed of portions. There are a variety of mathematical techniques available for working with numbers, both as wholes and in parts. Many of these techniques have broad application to higher mathematics, particularly in regard to simplifying expressions by common factoring.

For Further Research

Fractions are commonly used for denoting parts of a group, or portions of a whole. Why would having the ability to describe such mathematical situations be of use to people in ancient times? How do you suppose ancient cultures, which did not have a system of higher mathematics, were able to represent fractions in a non-numerical way? Consider the implications posed by the previous two questions, then try designing a system that portrays fractions using only visual symbols. Be sure to denote different denominators and methods for combining and reducing fractions. The system you devise can employ any combination of drawings, symbols, or pictures, but may not include words or numerals.

Name _____

Composite and Prime Numbers

Factoring is the process of finding all the factors of a number, essentially all the ways in which that number may be obtained from multiplication.

A **composite number** has additional factors beyond 1 and itself. An example of a composite number is 6, since its factors are 1, 2, 3, 6 (1 x 6 = 6 and 2 x 3 = 6).

A **prime number** has as factors the numbers 1 and itself. Prime numbers are difficult to work with in some applications since there is no way to break them down by factoring and canceling out like portions.

The following is a dependable method of determining factors. It involves simple inspection and works by exhausting each possibility until all factors are found.

Example: Find the factors of 36.

First, we know that 36 will have 1 and itself as factors. We also know that since 36 is an even number greater than 2, 2 will be one of its factors as well. So by inspection, 36 cannot be a prime number. We can write what we have already observed below.

(1, 2,   18, 36)

Begin filling in the other factors by asking questions. Try numbers in order until all possibilities have been exhausted. The next number to try is 3. Is 3 a factor of 36? If so, what number multiplied by 3 yields 36? At this point fill in 2 more factors.

(1, 2, 3,   12, 18, 36)

Next, is 4 a factor of 36? Yes, when multiplied by 9. Is 5 a factor? No. Fill in what has been learned.

(1, 2, 3, 4,   9, 12, 18, 3)

Next try 6. Six multiplied by itself is 36. We have now completed the factoring of this number since we have reached a perfect square.

Name _____

Composite and Prime Numbers (cont.)

While not all composite numbers have a perfect square, when you come to the point where a perfect square makes a larger number than the one you are factoring, you have found all the factors.

Find the factors of each of the numbers below. Write **prime** after the parenthesis if the number listed has only itself and 1 as factors.

1. 20   (   )

2. 39   (   )

3. 120   (   )

4. 17   (   )

5. 11   (   )

6. 64   (   )

7. 75   (   )

8. 48   (   )

9. 60   (   )

10. 41   (   )

11. 31   (   )

12. 200   (   )

 IF87128 *Standards-Based Math*

Name _____

Greatest Common Factors

What is the greatest common factor **(GCF)** of 16 and 24? First, find all the factors of each number.

16   (1, 2, 4, 8, 16)
24   (1, 2, 3, 4, 6, 8, 12, 24)

It is now easy to inspect both lists and look for common factors. While 16 and 24 have several factors in common, 8 is the greatest common factor.

Find the factors for each number group below, then determine the greatest common factor.

1.   28
      35
      GCF _____

2.   24
      30
      GCF _____

3.   45
      60
      GCF _____

4.   16
      48
      72
      GCF _____

5.   120
      160
      200
      GCF _____

6.   30
      45
      90
      GCF _____

Multiples

Being able to recognize multiples is important when working with fractions, bus schedules, monetary amounts, and other applications. Essentially, multiples are found by repeating the process of multiplication.

For example, the multiples of 6 are   6, 12, 18, 24, 30, 36, 42, 48, 54...

You can see that each multiple may be found by adding 6 at each interval or by multiplying 6 x 1, 6 x 2, 6 x 3, etc.

Find the least common multiple **(LCM)** by comparing the multiples of 2 or more numbers and determining which common multiple is the smallest.

Example: What is the least common multiple of 6 and 4? First, list the multiples of each number. Then compare the lists.

The multiples of 6 are 6, 12, 18, 24, 30...
The multiples of 4 are 4, 8, 12, 16, 20, 24, 28...

6 and 4 have several common multiples, but their LCM is 12.

Note that sometimes the LCM will be the product of the two numbers. Also, if one of the numbers is a multiple of the other, then the larger number is the LCM.

Determine the LCM for each of the number groups below.

1. For 8 and 10   LCM _____

2. For 6, 8, and 24   LCM _____

3. For 3 and 14   LCM _____

4. For 6, 12, and 30   LCM _____

5. For 7 and 12   LCM _____

6. For 5 and 30   LCM _____

7. For 40 and 60   LCM _____

8. For 10, 12, and 240   LCM _____

Name _____

More About GCF and LCM

Finding the greatest common factor or least common multiple can also be accomplished when variables are involved.

Example 1: What is the GCF of $10c$ and $24c$?

The factors of $10c$ are (c, 1, 2, 5, 10)
The factors of $24c$ are (c, 1, 2, 3, 4, 6, 8, 12, 24)
The GCF is $2c$.

Example 2: What is the LCM of $2a$ and $30a^2$?

Since 30 is a multiple of 2 and a^2 is a multiple of a, then $30a^2$ is the LCM.

Find the factors for each number group below, then determine the GCF.

1. $45y$ (   )
   $60y$ (   )
   GCF_____

2. $16r$ (   )
   $128r$ (   )
   GCF_____

3. 11 (   )
   $33k$ (   )
   $66k^2$ (   )
   GCF_____

4. $4r$ (   )
   $7kr$ (   )
   $17krt$ (   )
   GCF_____

Determine the LCM for each number group below.

5. 6 and $8y$ LCM_____

6. $5rt$ and $20t$ LCM_____

7. $50y$ and $100y^2$ LCM_____

Fractions: A Basic Part of the Math Process

Review Set

For the groups of fractions shown below, state the least common denominator.

1. $\frac{1}{7}, \frac{2}{12}$ LCD _____
2. $\frac{3}{16}, \frac{5}{8}$ LCD _____
3. $\frac{22}{24}, \frac{2}{16}$ LCD _____
4. $\frac{7}{8}, \frac{3}{5}, \frac{11}{20}$ LCD _____
5. $\frac{36}{36}, \frac{2}{3}, \frac{1}{6}$ LCD _____

6. $\frac{7}{10}, \frac{30}{40}$ LCD _____
7. $\frac{3}{5}, \frac{7}{9}$ LCD _____
8. $\frac{1}{31}, \frac{2}{3}$ LCD _____
9. $\frac{6}{7}, \frac{4}{9}, \frac{1}{2}$ LCD _____
10. $\frac{1}{205}, \frac{1}{10}$ LCD _____

Solve the problems below involving fractions. State answers as fully reduced fractions or as whole numbers with reduced fractions.

11. $\frac{1}{8} + \frac{2}{8} =$ _____
12. $\frac{3}{5} + \frac{4}{6} =$ _____
13. $\frac{1}{7} + \frac{1}{3} =$ _____
14. $1\frac{5}{8} + \frac{12}{7} =$ _____
15. $\frac{50}{3} + \frac{31}{7} =$ _____

16. $\frac{9}{12} - \frac{3}{12} =$ _____
17. $\frac{5}{6} - \frac{39}{60} =$ _____
18. $1 - \frac{5}{9} =$ _____
19. $\frac{4}{7} - \frac{1}{8} =$ _____
20. $2\frac{1}{8} - \frac{1}{2} =$ _____

Convert to decimal equivalents.

21. $\frac{7}{8} =$ _____
22. $\frac{3}{5} =$ _____
23. $\frac{1}{15} =$ _____
24. $\frac{30}{12} =$ _____
25. $3\frac{3}{13} =$ _____

Solve the problems below.

26. The floor layout of a particular room is rectangular in shape, 12" by 14". The floor has been tiled with 12-inch square tiles. One-fourth of the tiles are blue, and the remaining tiles are white. How many square feet of white tiles are in this room?

27. In a recent school election, 308 students voted. Seventy-two students voted for cartoon characters instead of the actual candidates. The other ballots were cast for students who were actually seeking office. What percentage of the students voted for actual candidates?

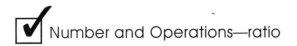

Name _____

Ratio

A **ratio** is essentially a size comparison of two numbers based on division. Look at the example below.

Example: There are twice as many boys in an after-school interpretive dance program as there are girls. This relationship (ratio) may be expressed in a number of ways. Perhaps the most common is the form:

$$2 : 1$$
$$(boys : girls)$$

There are other ways of stating this same ratio, such as with words "2 to 1" or as a fraction $\frac{2}{1}$.

Often a ratio may be solved by mental math, or by division if the multiples of numbers involved are not readily apparent. In the case of the interpretive dance class, if there are six boys in the class, there must be three girls if the ratio is correct. If there are eight boys, there will be four girls.

Answer each of the questions below involving ratio-related situations.

1. The students in a drama class follow a ratio of 2:9 boys to girls. If there are 18 girls in this class, how many boys are there?_____

2. A scale drawing shows the plans for a horse barn in a 1:48 ratio. If a wall of the horse barn on the plan is one foot in length, how many actual feet will that wall of the horse barn be?_____

3. A dessert recipe calls for 3 cups of flour and 1 cup of sugar. It serves 4 people. If the recipe must be altered to serve 12 people, how many cups of flour will be needed for the altered recipe?_____

Name _____

Ratio (cont.)

4. A restaurant has reserved seats for smokers and nonsmokers in a 1:12 ratio. If there are only 10 seats for smokers, how many seats are reserved for nonsmokers?_____

5. A theater manager noticed that the ratio of people viewing comedy movies as compared to the number of people viewing action movies is 5:3. If 200 people watch comedies, how many watch action movies? _____

6. A car model is listed on the box as being 1:36 scale. If a piece on the model is exactly one inch in length, how many feet would the actual piece be on a full-sizedcar?_____

7. A doctor has noticed there are 240 patients in a hospital with health insurance, while 60 patients are without health insurance. What is a simplified ratio to express the number of insured patients to the number without insurance?_____

8. The computer chips produced at a factory come through the manufacturing process with a set portion of unusable chips. The ratio of usable to unusable chips is 18:1. If 500 unusable chips were produced in one day, how many usable chips were produced?_____

9. A particular outboard motor needs oil to gasoline in a ratio of 1:32. How many ounces of oil should be added to a gallon of gasoline?_____

10. If one-fifth of teenagers fail the first time they take their drivers-license test, how many teenagers might reasonably be expected to fail if 15 have signed up for the test on a particular Saturday morning?_____

11. An artist had prints produced of his favorite painting. The original painting is 36 inches in length by 24 inches in width. He will produce 1,000 prints. If the prints are to be two-thirds the size of the original, what are the dimensions of each print?_____

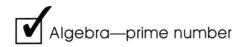

Name _____

The Elusive and Mysterious Prime Number

Consider the situations below involving prime numbers. In some you may need to test a hypothesis or consider an abstract concept. Write a few paragraphs or a short paper to describe your findings.

1. Of the first 10 integers, 4 are prime numbers. There are 25 prime numbers among the first 100 integers. Prime numbers become more scarce as numbers become larger. Why do you think that is?

2. For every integer that can be named, add 1 and a larger integer is produced. This is the nature of an infinite series. Even though extremely large prime numbers are difficult to find, computers have found prime numbers with thousands of digits. What argument could you pose to someone who sees a new large prime number listed in a math journal and says, "This must surely be the biggest prime number!"

3. The following two formulas will produce prime numbers. Try testing the following formulas by inserting some sample values for x.

   $$x^2 + x + 41 \qquad\qquad x^2 + x + 17$$

   Did you encounter any composite numbers using formulas. If you did, it illustrates why these formulas do not predict all prime numbers. While the formulas generate many prime numbers by inserting different x values, neither formula is perfect, and both will produce composite numbers. Why do you think there are no known formulas for producing all the prime numbers?

Name _____

Geometry

Euclid, a Greek mathematician living nearly 2,300 years ago, compiled much of what was known about geometry at the time into a series of 13 books known as *Euclid's Elements*. Not much is known about Euclid. He may have been an important teacher in ancient Alexandria during the reign of Ptolemy. Euclid wove his own knowledge of geometry into his books and borrowed from the works of others. The result was a treatise on basic geometry that has endured the test of time.

The 13 books that comprise *Euclid's Elements* are organized as follows: Books 1 through 4 present simple plane geometric figures. Book 5 relates to proportions and ratios. Book 6 touches on the Pythagorean Theorem and similar figures. Books 7 through 9 deal with number theory. Book 10 covers lengths and square roots and their effects in geometric computations. Books 11 through 13 address the geometry of solid figures. These books represented a comprehensive work for the time, and literally spread throughout the world. Euclid's original work can no longer be precisely traced as the work was copied, edited, and added to at various times over the centuries. Today Euclid is credited as being the "Father of Geometry."

The activities in this section are built around the concept that geometric figures have a greater scope than that of simply applying formulas to compute areas or perimeters. Geometry forms the basic building blocks of our three-dimensional world, and its implications are evident everywhere. In this section geometry is presented as a body of knowledge rather than a subset of mathematics.

For Further Research
Much attention is paid to the academic work of the ancient Greeks and Romans. The European and American cultures were influenced by these cultures. What was happening in other parts of the world in terms of learning and the arts during the period that spanned from 1000 B.C. through A.D. 1000? China, India, and parts of the Middle East were experiencing ages of enlightenment and learning during this time. Select a time period or a geographic region and learn about the people and discoveries. Organize your findings into a short paper or use your notes to develop an oral report.

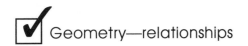

Name _____

The Earth Is Flat

Over one hundred years ago a somewhat controversial geometry book was published in England. The author of this book was Edwin Abbott, and the book was titled *Flatland*.

Flatland was not a geometry book in the sense that it was intended to teach mathematics. The book was intended to be a commentary on England's somewhat stuffy, traditional social class system of the period. Abbott made the characters in his book geometric figures, each having its role and status in society determined by its number of sides. Multisided polygons were at the top of the social ladder, while line segments and triangles with one especially short side (isosceles) were at the bottom. The most perfect citizen would be a polygon with so many short sides that it neared the shape of a circle.

Abbott was concerned by the limited role of women in British society, as well as the plight of the lower classes. Education, particularly at the university level, was reserved almost entirely for males of the upper and upper middle classes. Women were expected to run a household or to work in a menial occupation. They did not have the right to vote. In *Flatland*, women were depicted as line segments, an attempt by Abbott to illustrate that the capabilities of women as a whole were being ignored.

Quite appropriately, the characters in *Flatland* exist in two-dimensional space. (Our own world is, of course, three-dimensional.) Two-dimensional space might be easily compared to a tabletop where cutout paper shapes such as triangles, squares, or pentagons may be moved about freely but may not be stacked upon each other. If you were one of these figures, you would never be able to observe another figure in its entirety. Abbott used this comparison to illustrate that many people in English society were not seen for their potential capabilities but were seen only in the context of their positions in this limited class system.

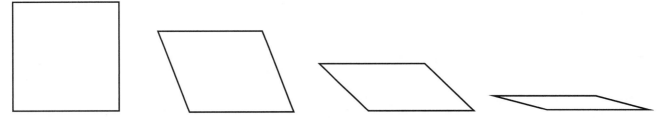

The figure on the left is a square as seen from a front view. Imagine the square being pushed over. The square would then appear as a line segment. This is the way in which the square would be viewed by a resident of Flatland.

IF87128 *Standards-Based Math*

The Earth Is Flat (cont.)

One day the world of Flatland is turned upside down when a sphere visits one of its residents. The visiting sphere demonstrates the truth of another dimension by passing through Flatland as an expanding and diminishing circle. The residents of Flatland were not ready to accept this truth. In this way, Abbott was clearly drawing a parallel to the slow changes a society makes when confronted with the need for social change.

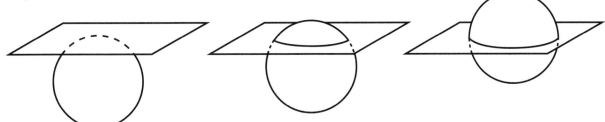

This drawing depicts a sphere as it passes through a plane surface. The view of this sphere to a resident of Flatland would have only been that portion of the sphere intersecting the plane at that particular moment. The sphere would appear to be a curve of varying widths.

Select one of the projects described below for further research.

I. Can you think of other examples in which literature or film has attempted to draw attention to a particular social issue? Select a work and write a short paper describing how it may have promoted a particular social-related cause or position. (The work you select does not necessarily have to use a mathematics application as the vehicle for telling its story.)

II. Why do you think the residents of Flatland were well-suited for demonstrating a class system? Can you think of other examples in which fictional characters possessed traits that were particularly well-suited for the type of work or the cause in which they were involved? Think of a few examples for discussion or write a short paper to describe your choices.

III. Imagine a world similar to Flatland where all the inhabitants are geometric figures such as pyramids, cubes, and cylinders. How would the interests and needs of these citizens be different from one another? What type of candidates would such figures be inclined to vote for in elections? Would cubes only want other cubes for candidates? What kind of chairs would cylinders want at movie theaters? Would pyramids approve? Write a fictional story or short play about this world of geometric figures.

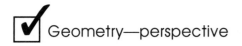

Name _____

Geometric Figures—A Different Perspective

Geometric figures are often seen depicted in a particular way. Look at the typical drawing of a cube shown below.

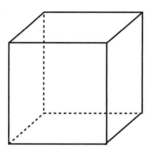

Now look at these two illustrations.

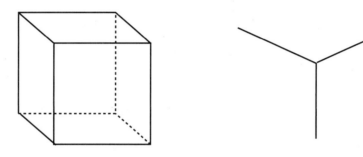

The illustration on the left is a view of the cube as it might be seen from above at a position slightly off to the side of the cube. On the right is a view from the inside of the cube, as might be seen from the center of the cube looking up at one of the corners.

Draw these figures below from two different perspectives. You may choose any view. Write a short caption under each of your drawings describing the perspective you have chosen. Use the example above.

1.

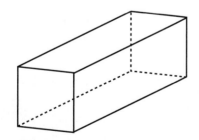

Name _____

Geometric Figures—A Different Perspective (cont.)

2.

3.

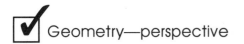

Name _____

More About Perspective

Let us look at geometric figures from yet another perspective. When a knife cuts through a grapefruit at the center, we are left with two halves. The place where the spherical grapefruit was cut is nearly circular.

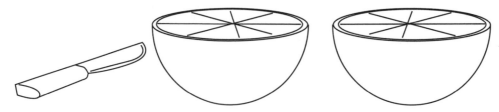

If we cut through another figure as shown below, we are left with a shape much different from that above. A square would be the cross section of this pyramid at the place where the plane intersects it.

For each of the figures below, draw the shape at the point where the plane intersects it.

1.

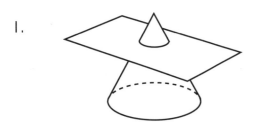

2.

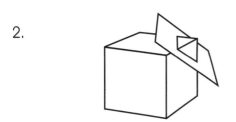

Name _____

More About Perspective (cont.)

3.

4.

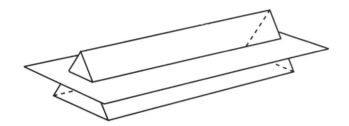

5.

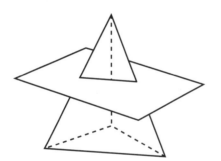

6.

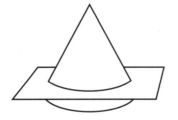

Name _____

Wrap It Up, and I'll Take It

Geometric figures may be unwrapped to reveal their component shapes by cutting the figures at their seams. A cylinder, when unfolded, would appear as a rectangle and two circles.

 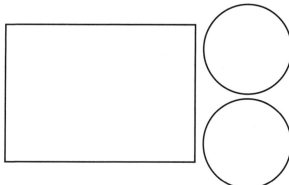

Sometimes a figure is easier to analyze if the component shapes can be more readily seen. Some computations, such as finding the surface area, are more easily accomplished if the figure can be seen in parts.

For each of the figures shown below, create a drawing to depict the figure as if it were unfolded at the seams.

1.

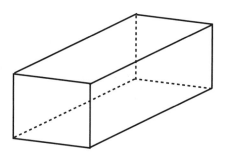

2.

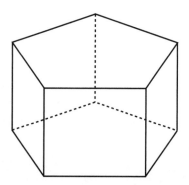

Name _____

Wrap It Up, and I'll Take It (cont.)

3.

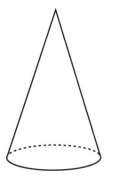

4.

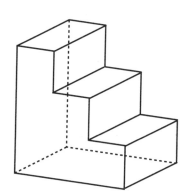

5.

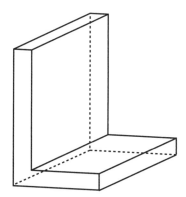

6.

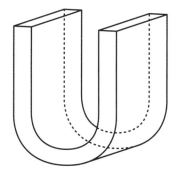

Knowing Your Way Around

The **perimeter** of a regular or irregular polygon is the distance around its outside edges. That distance is found by computing the sum of its sides.

The **circumference** of a circle can be likened to the perimeter of a polygon. The formula for circumference is $C = \pi d$, or $C = 2\pi r$.

Compute the perimeter or circumference of each figure.

1. A rectangle with a long side of 24 cm and a short side of 14 cm _____

2. A hexagon with sides of $3\frac{3}{4}$ inches _____

3. A circle with a diameter of 60 meters _____

4. A rectangular that is 120 feet on one side and $20\frac{1}{3}$ yards on the other side _____

5. A pentagon that has $\frac{1}{4}$ of its interior shaded, with all sides 3.5 inches _____

Solve the problems involving perimeter and circumference.

6. Trey made a large circular region using a rope. The region has a diameter of $12\frac{2}{3}$ feet. How many feet of rope did Trey have available?

   _____

7. Janelle is building a pen to house her rabbits. The pen will be rectangular and will have the back of the barn as one of its longer sides. Janelle has planned to have 180 square feet of space within the pen, with the short sides of the pen each measuring 6 feet. How much fencing material will she need?

   _____

8. Sharon is building a circular brick path in her garden. Sharon knows the project will take four weekends to finish since she can only complete a section of the walkway at a time. The circular path will have a diameter of 40 feet once completed. How many feet of walkway should she be able to finish the first weekend?

   _____

Name _____

Open Spaces

Area is a measure of the size of a surface or of a flat expanse.

Several formulas are shown below.

Rectangle (to include squares):   A = length x width
                                    A = **l w**

Triangle: A = $\frac{1}{2}$ x base x height
                                    A = $\frac{1}{2}$**bh**

Circle: A = $\pi\mathbf{r}^2$

Compute the area for each of the regular figures described below. You may find it helpful to draw a diagram.

1. A rectangle with sides of 20 inches and 40 inches _____

2. A square with sides of 7 cm _____

3. A triangle with a base of $3\frac{1}{2}$ inches and a height of $6\frac{1}{4}$ inches _____

4. A circle with a radius of 6 meters _____

5. The portion of a 16 inch by 16 inch square that is not covered by a circle. The circle has a radius of 3 inches and has been placed in the center of the square. _____

6. The total area formed by a triangle with a base of $4\frac{1}{4}$ inches and a height of 10 inches and rectangle that is 10 inches by $4\frac{1}{4}$ inches _____

         IF87128 *Standards-Based Math*

Name _____

Open Spaces (cont.)

Solve the problems involving areas. You may find it helpful to draw a diagram.

7. Rachel has staked out a rectangular region for planting a garden. The region is 50 feet long by $12\frac{1}{2}$ feet wide. She plans to use one-fifth of the garden's overall area for flowers. How many square feet of garden will be used for flowers?

_____

8. Acme-Ace Garage Parking Facility has three levels available for parking cars. Each level is rectangular in shape and measures 220 feet by 80 feet. On each level, 22.5% of the available area is used for ramps, driveways, and other special zones. How much floor space does Acme-Ace have available for parking vehicles? _____

9. The tin roof of Carolyn's vacation house was damaged. The roof is composed of two large sections that are rectangular in shape and adjoin at the roof peak. Each of these two large sections measures 60 feet by 36 feet.

A. What is the total area of the roof on Carolyn's vacation house?_____

B. The piece of her roof that was damaged and needs replacing measures 3 feet by 12 feet. What percentage of the whole roof does this piece represent?_____

10. A teacher has decided that the circular-shaped parachute used for recess should be trimmed and resewn. The parachute is currently 60 feet in diameter. She plans to trim $1\frac{1}{2}$ feet off the outside edge all the way around. What will be the area of this parachute once it has been trimmed?_____

11. Walt purchased a roll of carpet that measured 60 square yards. Walt paid $220.00 for this roll of carpet. How much did Walt pay per square yard?_____

Name _____

More About Area

It is possible to estimate the area of an irregular figure by using a simple technique involving grid work. Look at the figures below. In Figure B, each grid square defines a 1-unit space. By counting all the grids occupied by the figure and adding the ones that are only partially covered, an estimate for the number of square units may be obtained.

Figure A

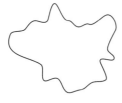

Figure B

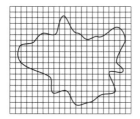

1. For the figure shown below, draw a 1-centimeter grid work and tally an estimate for the area of the figure.

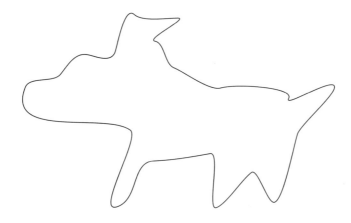

Area Estimate _____

Name _____

More About Area (cont.)

2. For the figure shown below, draw a 1-inch grid work and tally an estimate for the figure's area.

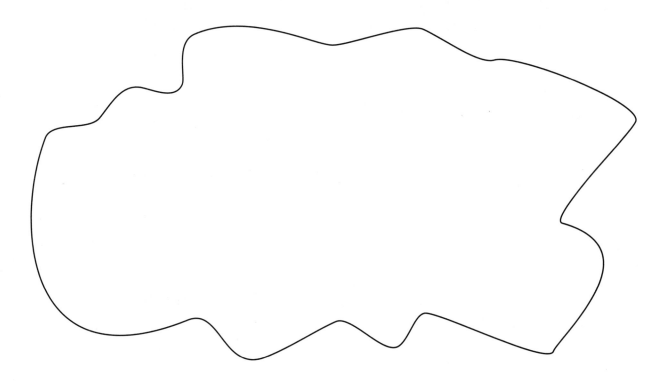

Area Estimate _____

Short Answer

3. Do you think a smaller grid work yields a better estimate for the area of a figure? Why or why not?

4. What factors, aside from the size of the grid work, might influence the accuracy of an estimate for the areas of irregular figures?

Name _____

Inside Out

Imagine the inside of an enclosed space such as a traffic cone, a cardboard box, or one of the ancient pyramids of Egypt. The interior space of an object is its **volume**. The volumes of many standard figures may be easily found using formulas.

Rectangular Prism (including cubes):
$\quad v$ = length x width x height
$\quad v$ = **lwh**

Square or Rectangular Pyramid:
$\quad v = \frac{1}{3}$ x (area of base) x height
$\quad v = \frac{1}{3}$ x $\quad$ (l x w) $\quad$ x $\quad h$
$\quad v = \frac{1}{3}$**lwh**

Cylinder:
$\quad v$ = (area of base) x height
$\quad v = \pi r^2 \quad$ x $\quad h$
$\quad v = \pi$ **r²h**

Cone:
$\quad v$ = (area of base) x height
$\quad v = (\frac{1}{3}\pi r^2) \quad$ x $\quad h$
$\quad v = \frac{1}{3}\pi$ **r²h**

Sphere:
$\quad v = \frac{4}{3}\pi$ **r²**

Compute the volume for each of the regular figures described below.

1. A rectangular prism with a height of 3 cm, a width of 3 cm, and a length of 12 cm

   _____

2. A square pyramid with a base of 6 inches by 6 inches and a height of 6 inches

   _____

3. A cylinder with a height of 40 cm and a radius of 5 cm _____

4. A cone-shaped water cup with a height of 12 cm and a radius of 8 cm _____

5. A rectangular-shaped storage shed with interior dimensions of 12 feet by 8 feet by 8 feet _____

Name _____

Inside Out (cont.)

Rewrite each of the volume-related formulas into a simplified algebraic form, depending on the figures involved.

6. The formula of a rectangular prism changed to describe only a cube with sides of q. _____

7. The formula of a pyramid changed to describe only a square-based pyramid with sides of y. _____

8. The formula of a cylinder changed to describe a cylinder whose height is the same measure as its radius. _____

9. The formula for the portion of a cylinder not occupied when a smaller cone is stored inside the cylinder. _____

Solve the volume-related problems below.

10. Griffin took a storage box with a height of 20 inches and cut off a 4-inch strip all the way around, thereby reducing the height of the box. If the box had been capable of holding 2,000 cubic inches of material before the strip was removed, how much can it now hold?_____

11. Joanne is planning to move to a new apartment. She has the choice of buying a cylindrical container for packing dishes and glassware or of buying a similarly sized rectangular box. The cylinder drum's interior is 40 inches tall with a radius of 11 inches. The box's interior is 36 inches tall with both a length and width of 24 inches. Which box has more storage space and by how much?_____

12. Ralph wants to buy a dishwasher. The problem is that the counter where it must be installed is only $32\frac{3}{4}$ inches deep. The dishwasher with the closest matching depth is $34\frac{1}{8}$ inches from back to front. Its height is 34 inches and its width is 30 inches, both of these measures being within the limits of the space available. If installed, how much of this dishwasher will stick out beyond the counter?

_____

Name _____

Surface Area

You have learned that 3-dimensional figures can be "unfolded" and laid flat. This concept shows the surface area of such figures. Formulas for area can then be applied to each section of the unfolded figure. The total surface area is the sum of each of the sections. Study the example below, showing an unfolded cube with 5-inch sides. For this cube the area of each section is 25 square inches. Total surface area of this cube would be 150 square inches.

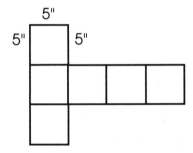

For each of the figures below, make a sketch of the "unfolded" figure and then determine its surface area.

1. A rectangular prism with sides of 12 inches by 24 inches by 36 inches

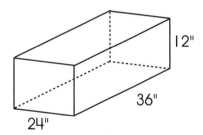

2. A cylinder with height of $10\frac{1}{2}$ centimeters and radius of $2\frac{1}{4}$ centimeters

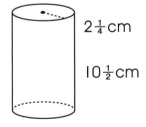

3. A cube with sides of $\frac{2}{3}$ inches

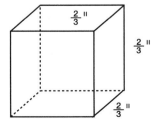

                   IF87128 *Standards-Based Math*

The Pythagorean Theorem

The **Pythagorean Theorem** applies to the lengths of the sides of a right triangle. It is not really known who first discovered this practical formula. The Greek mathematician Pythagoras, however, has been loosely linked to this theorem.

A right triangle has one angle that measures 90 degrees. The Pythagorean Theorem provides a formula for solving for the length of an unknown side when the lengths of the other two sides are known.

The formula is shown below for the "3-4-5 triangle."

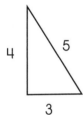

For right triangles, the square of the longest side of the triangle (hypotenuse) will equal the sum of the squares of the two shorter sides.

$$a^2 + b^2 = c^2$$

Now try the values for the triangle above.

$$3^2 + 4^2 = 5^2$$
$$9 + 16 = 25$$

This concept can be demonstrated using areas as well. You can see from this illustration that 9 units + 16 units = 25 units.

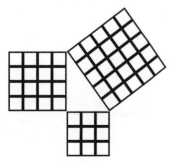

                   IF87128 *Standards-Based Math*

Name _____

The Pythagorean Theorem (cont.)

For each of the number groups listed, use the Pythagorean Theorem to determine which groups could represent the sides of a right triangle. Write "Yes" or "No" in the blanks provided.

1. _____ 5, 12, 13   5. _____ 9, 13, 15
2. _____ 6, 8, 10   6. _____ 5, 6, 7
3. _____ 7, 24, 25   7. _____ 9, 12, 15
4. _____ 12, 16, 20   8. _____ 3, 5, 8

Use the Pythagorean Theorem to assist in solving the problems below. Some problems will involve finding the square root of imperfect squares, so you may wish to use a calculator.

9. The base of an extendable ladder is positioned 4 feet away from a wall. The top of the ladder is touching a point on the wall that is 10 feet above the ground. To what length has the ladder been extended? _____

10. A gate that is rectangular with dimensions of 4 feet long by 3 feet high has a piece of wire tightened across it diagonally in order to strengthen the gate. How long is that diagonal? _____

11. The driver of a car began a trip by traveling 30 miles due west, then turned due north and drove 40 miles. At this point how far was the car from its starting point in terms of actual distance? _____

12. A ramp used for loading heavy cargos into trucks has been constructed in the shape of a right triangle. The height of the ramp is 36 inches. The base of this ramp is 48 inches. How long is the inclined portion of the ramp? _____

Short Answer

13. What do you think is the main drawback of the Pythagorean Theorem?

Name _____

More About the Pythagorean Theorem

Evidence suggests the Pythagorean Theorem was actually known to ancient scholars many centuries before the time of Pythagoras. The Babylonians may have solved this early mathematics mystery 1,000 years before Pythagoras was born. A clay tablet of ancient Babylon, now archived at a prominent New York University, contains the proof—mathematical calculations related to right triangles.

Pythagoras may have learned of the special properties of the right triangle from studying with the Egyptians. Some 2,500 years ago, Pythagoras founded a school in the southern portion of what is now Italy.

Pythagoras' school was founded on the study of mathematics. The 3-4-5 right triangle was considered of special importance to the school. Pythagoras, or his students, contributed much to what would later become *Euclid's Elements*, an important early Greek treatise on geometry.

For Further Research
Throughout history, many discoveries have been attributed to one person, when another, or others should receive the credit. Columbus is credited as being the first European to discover America, although Vikings had settlements in North America hundreds of years before Columbus. Although a prominent German scientist, Gotfried Wilhelm Leibniz, may be the rightful father of calculus, Isaac Newton receives the credit.

Investigate a prominent person, discovery, or event in history. Your project could center around the work of an inventor or an explorer. It could focus on the evolution of an invention. In your research, pay close attention to the people involved, the timeline of events, and the means by which the event was chronicled and credit assigned. Organize your thoughts into a paper or an oral presentation.

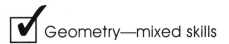

Name _____

More Work with Geometry

Solve the problems below involving various geometric applications.

1. A circular jogging trail at a large park is ¾ mile from beginning to end. An area with benches, water fountains, and restrooms has been constructed at the center of this circular track. While a jogger is using this circular jogging track, how far is she at any given time from the facilities at the center of this track? _____

2. Bonnie is planning to carry a rectangular poster at a demonstration. She is has the choice of poster board in two sizes. The larger poster board has dimensions of 56 cm by 76 cm. The smaller poster board has dimensions of 35 cm by 50 cm.
   A. Although the smaller poster board is easier to carry, how many more square centimeters of area per side does the larger poster offer? _____
   B. The larger poster board is priced at $3.89 while the smaller poster board is priced at $2.89. Which board represents a better cost per square centimeter? _____

3. A box with dimensions of 18 inches by 18 inches by 24 inches is full of loose plastic packing material shaped like peanuts.
   A. Would a cylindrical container that is 26 inches tall with a radius of 8 inches be large enough to hold all of the packing material? _____
   B. What is the difference in capacity between the two containers? _____

4. Casey is buying a group of solar power panels. He knows that a minimum of 24 square feet of panels are needed for generating the power he needs. The panels come in 2 sizes: 18 inches by 30 inches and 24 inches by 36 inches.
   A. If he buys the smaller-sized panels, how many will he need? _____
   B. If he buys the larger-sized panels, how many will he need? _____

Short Answer
5. Evan has three sections of boards that he plans to nail together into a frame in the shape of a right triangle. The boards have the following lengths: 8 feet, 5 feet, 6 feet. Can a right triangle be made from these boards and, if so, what would be the maximum length possible for the hypotenuse?

Name _____

Coordinate Plane Graphing

A **coordinate plane** provides grid work for specifying locations in a visual format. Those locations are specified by an (x, y) coordinate pair.

Look at the simple equation y = 2x. By taking several x values (such as x = 1, 2, 3, 4) and plugging these values into the equation one at a time, corresponding y values can be determined, thereby providing a coordinate pair. For example, when x is 1, the value of y is 2. When x is 2, the value of y is 4. When x is 3, the value of y is 6. And when x is 4, the value of y is 8. Coordinate pairs for each of these groups of points can then be made: (1, 2) (2, 4) (3, 6) (4, 8). These points can be plotted on an appropriate graph.

Use the graph below to answer the questions. Depending on the information given, provide either a point or a coordinate pair.

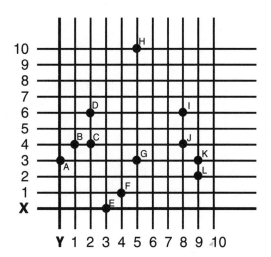

1. G (,)

2. K (,)

3. B (,)

4. A (,)

5. (9, 2) _____

6. (2, 4) _____

7. (4, 1) _____

8. (8, 4) _____

IF87128 *Standards-Based Math*

Name _____

Coordinate Plane Graphing (cont.)

Use the graph on page 68 and your knowledge of geometry to answer the following.

9. What is the area of the rectangle formed by points D, C, J, I? _____

10. If points H and I form a hypotenuse for a triangle whose third point is located at (5, 6), then compute the area of this triangle. _____

11. What is the length of the hypotenuse described in problem 10? _____

12. What coordinate pair would form a rectangle when associated with points G, K, L?

_____

13. Which two points have the most distance between them compared to all the other points indicated on this graph? _____

14. Name the points that are found at $y = 4$ on this graph. _____

15. Do the points on this graph appear to represent an equation, such as $y = 2x$? Why or why not?

16. Suppose this graph actually represents a salesperson's territory. The x-axis indicates Elm Street, and the y-axis is Oak Street. If the points represent households who have previously bought merchandise, can any conclusions be drawn from the information presented?

17. What conclusion might you draw if the graph represented robberies of convenience stores in a neighborhood, and you were studying the graph as a detective? Would the information become more relevant if only the convenience store had not been robbed at coordinates (6, 2) What can you say about the information in the graph given in this context compared with the situation described in problem 16 of a salesperson's territory?

More About Coordinate Plane Graphing

The coordinate plane extends beyond the single quadrant where values of both x and y are positive. Look at the example below that names each of the quadrants and shows points plotted in each.

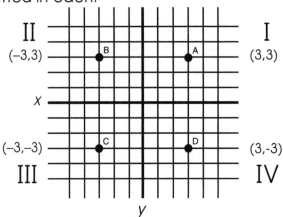

This example shows that a negative x-value will always describe a point on the left side of the y-axis. A negative y value will always describe a point below the x-axis. When both x and y values are negative, it will always describe a point in quadrant III.

For each of the coordinate points below, give the corresponding quadrants.

1. (3, –5) _____
2. (2, 7) _____
3. (–4, –8) _____
4. (2, –3) _____

5. (–2, 3) _____
6. (–4, 1) _____
7. (–5,–5) _____
8. (–4, 1) _____

9. In the space below, draw a coordinate plane and plot the following points:
   T (–4, 3)   R (–4, 1)   V (–4, –2)   W (–4, –4)

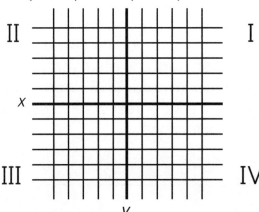

10. Study the points you plotted in question 9. Would an equation define the locations of these points? Experiment with the x and y values to determine what the equation for these points would be.

Name _____

More About Coordinate Plane Graphing (cont.)

For the linear functions below, determine enough x and y values to plot the line on a coordinate plane.

11. $y = 2x + 1$

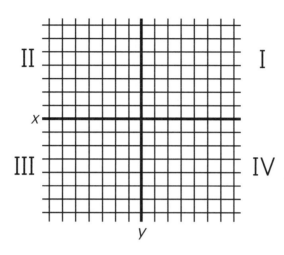

12. $y = 5x - 3$

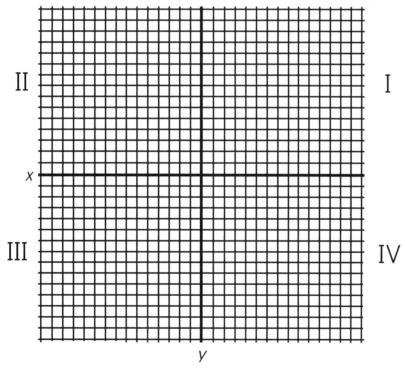

13. In problem 11, at what coordinates does the line cross the y-axis? _____
Set the x-value at zero as a quick means of finding the intercept.

14. In problem #12, at what coordinates does the line cross the y-axis? _____
Set the x-value at zero as a quick means of finding the intercept.

     IF87128 *Standards-Based Math*

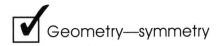

Name _____

Lines of Symmetry

A **line of symmetry** is drawn through a figure if the portions of the figure on each side of the line match exactly. Look at the examples below.

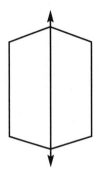

If you think of the line of symmetry drawn as an axis line over which each side of the figure could be flipped, then it is clear that the hexagon above is symmetrical, but the figure at the bottom of the page is not.

Some symmetrical figures will have many lines of symmetry, while others have a single line of symmetry. In the case of the hexagon above, a number of lines can be drawn that will produce lines of symmetry, as shown below.

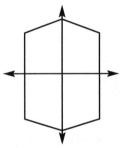

Some items, that at first glance would appear symmetrical, are not truly symmetrical. Consider the example of a handblown glass vase. It might appear to be symmetrical, but since the vase was not made in a conforming mold of perfect dimensions it will probably be somewhat lopsided. Sometimes these subtle differences are not readily apparent to the human eye.

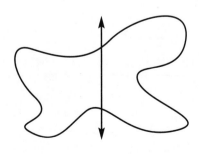

People's faces are another good example. If you study the picture of someone's face, you will see that a line drawn down his or her forehead through the bridge of the nose reveals differences on each side of this line. Some computer programs can illustrate this by pasting together two left sides or two right sides of the same face. The result tends to look like a different person.

Name _____

Lines of Symmetry (cont.)

For each of the figures shown below, indicate whether the line drawn is a line of symmetry by writing "Yes" or "No" in the blanks provided.

1._____

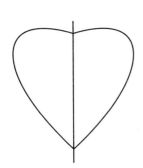

2._____

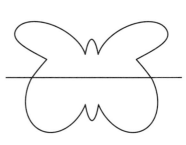

3._____

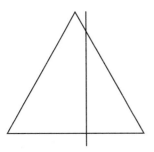

4._____

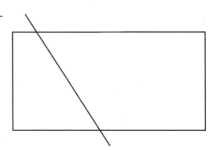

5._____

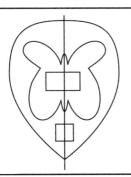

6._____

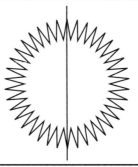

7._____

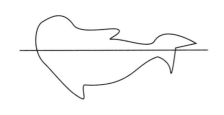

8._____

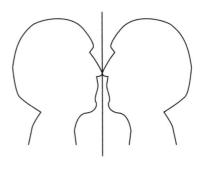

Name _____

Rotation Around an Axis

When a figure is rotated around an axis, it creates a solid, where only a two-dimensional figure had previously existed. Look at the illustration below.

If the circle shown in the illustration above were spun around the axis line as indicated, a figure resembling a solid ring would be created, similar in appearance to the illustration shown below.

For each of the figures shown below, draw a sketch of that figure as it would look after being rotated around the axis as indicated.

1.

2.

3.

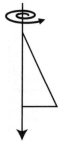

4.

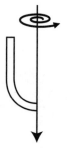

IF87128 *Standards-Based Math*

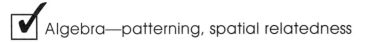

The Famous Map Coloring Problem

A mapmaker in 1850s England discovered that he needed only four different colors to color a map of all the counties in England. The mapmaker, Francis Guthrie, found that four colors were all that was needed to ensure that counties (or regions) with adjacent borders were not the same color and could therefore be easily differentiated.

In the 1970s, a proof was constructed by mathematicians, showing that four colors were indeed enough to color any map. However, the proof used computers in an area where mathematicians insist that human minds must be able to verify all results. More work on the unique map-coloring problem has verified that four colors are enough, but producing a proof that is acceptable to all of academia remains elusive.

The basic rules for the map-coloring problem are simple. Adjacent map regions may not use the same color, but colors may meet at a point without being counted as adjoining. For instance, if four rectangular regions meet at a common point, that corner point may be touched by the same color.

1. Shade the figure below using the fewest colors possible.

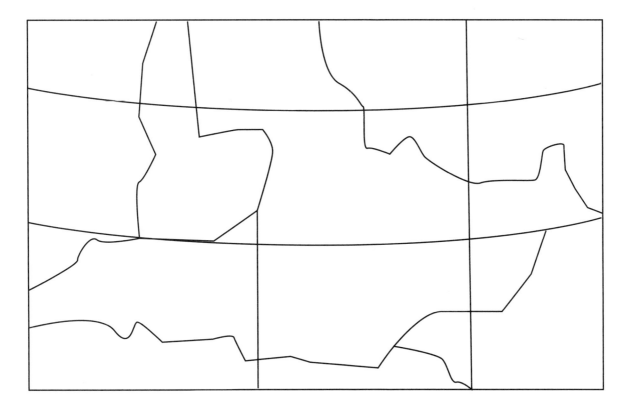

The Famous Map Coloring Problem (cont.)

2. In the space below draw a basic map region that would need only three colors and still follow the rules of the map-coloring problem.

3. In the space below, construct a map region that needs five colors to complete the coloring pattern.

For Discussion

4. In your testing of the map-coloring problems, did it seem to make a difference which region you began coloring, or how many total regions there were on the map? If not, could this be a factor in the number of colors needed for other map-coloring situations?

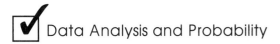
Practical Matters

Algebra was loosely named for an Arabian text written about 1,200 years ago titled *Hisab al-jabr w' al-muqabala.* The title translates to "Calculation by Restoration and Reduction." These formulas were designed for use with trade and commerce transactions.

Rene Descartes, a French mathematician of the 1600s, published *La Geometrie* in 1637. His work was the first to blend the Euclidian style of basic figures geometry with modern algebra used for describing and computing the figures. This major work formed the basis for what is now modern analytic geometry.

By the late 1600s, Europe had rekindled its interest in the sciences and in mathematics. In this age of discovery, Gottfried Wilhelm Leibniz and Sir Isaac Newton were battling over credit for the discovery of calculus. While a definitive answer to the question may never be known, it is widely thought that calculus may have been first used by Sir Isaac Newton in private research papers and then separately developed by both men on their own. While the calculus used today more closely resembles the work of Leibniz, Newton may indeed have been the first to utilize it.

The activities in this section take a look back through the practical side of mathematics. Mathematics is found everywhere in our daily lives. From the supermarket checkout to the post office, we make mathematics decisions every day. Many of these decisions require a blend of life experience with mathematical knowledge.

For Further Research
Try keeping a journal for one week detailing all mathematics-related decisions and observations you make. Be on the lookout not only for monetary decisions but for mathematics in the kitchen, library, sports field, and other places. Think about how decisions you made differed from those of your classmates. Share your findings by creating a graph or present your findings as an oral report.

Miles Per Gallon

Miles per gallon, or mpg, simply refers to how far a car, on average, can travel on one gallon of fuel. Calculating the mpg is a function of division. The basic formula is:

Miles Driven ÷ Number of Gallons Used = mpg rating

Example: George bought a vintage "muscle car." On the way home, he filled the gas tank of his car and noted the mileage at 109,912. A few days later, after not having driven the car very much, George noticed the fuel tank gauge was nearly empty. Once again he stopped at the gas station and put 22 gallons of gas in the car's tank. At this point he noted the mileage was 110,164. How does George determine the mpg rating for his car?

Miles Driven	÷	Number of Gallons Used	=	mpg rating
(109,912 – 110,164)	÷	22	=	mpg rating
252	÷	22	=	mpg rating
	11.45		=	mpg rating

George's new car averages 11.45 miles per gallon of gas used.

Compute the mpg figure for each of the situations described below.

1. Jackie's motorcycle went 228 miles on $4\frac{1}{5}$ gallons of gas.
   mpg _____

2. Annie's truck went 184.8 miles on 12.5 gallons of fuel.
   mpg _____

3. Mr. James is testing a new vehicle for possible use as a company fleet car. He began driving the car with a full tank of gas, testing it on the highway and in the city to get the best possible data for his test. The car's odometer showed 15 when the trip began. The odometer read 185 when the test was concluded. At that time, the car's fuel tank accepted only 4.8 gallons of gas.
   mpg _____

Miles Per Gallon (cont.)

Answer the questions below relating to mpg ratings and fuel costs.

4. Porter Moving Company operates a truck that gets 12 mpg on average. If the expected cost of fuel is $2.39 per gallon, how much will a trip of 412 miles cost?

   _____

5. Helga's car got 12 kilometers per liter of fuel before she took her car in for maintenance. This maintenance was overdue, and Helga noticed an immediate 20% increase in her car's fuel efficiency. How many kilometers per liter is her car now getting?

   _____

6. Arnie manages a fleet of trucks for a utility company. The utility's total cost for fuel during the previous year was $17,588. Utility trucks were driven a total of 106,800 miles during the previous year. What is the average cost per mile for the fuel used?

   _____

7. Julian has a car that gets 14.44 mpg on average. He's planning to buy a new car that is rated at 22 mpg. Last year Julian used his car a lot, driving 18,200 miles. He thinks he would use the new car just as much. Julian predicts gasoline will cost him an average of $1.90 per gallon during the coming year. If his assumptions are correct, how much money would Julian save on fuel costs in the coming year by buying the new car?

   _____

8. An automobile mechanic has been tinkering with a car engine, trying to improve its efficiency. He's found that this engine will idle for 1 hour, using only $\frac{3}{4}$ gallon of gas. How long should the engine idle on 1 gallon of gas?

   _____

Short Answer

9. MPG figures provide an average, essentially an approximation based on information collected. What factors might contribute to mpg figures not being accurate or even unreliable?

   _____

Math in Aisle 5—Cleanup at the Register

Solve the problems below involving grocery store situations and consumer math.

1. Lisa noticed that a 12-pack of her favorite soda costs $2.99. Near the cash register in a refrigerated case she saw single cans of the same soda for sale at $0.79 each. She bought two 12-packs of the soda. How many more cans does she get for the money she spent than if she had purchased single cans?

    _____

2. Jennifer works in the produce department at a local supermarket. She thinks the manager of the produce department is always trying to cheat the customers by not pricing things clearly. For example, fresh mushrooms were sold the previous week for $3.29 per pound. This week the same mushrooms are being sold only in prepackaged quantities of 4 ounces. The cost of these packaged mushrooms is $0.99 per pack. How much more expensive per pound are the mushrooms this week than last week?

    _____

3. Herbert always assumed that jumbo-sized products were more economical to buy. For example, an 8-pound box of his favorite laundry detergent costs $8.99. Out of curiosity, Herbert decided to compare what he was paying per ounce for the 8-pound box with the cost per ounce of the 5-pound box. If the 5-pound box costs $4.89, how much more per ounce does it cost to buy the larger size?

    _____

4. Lin noticed that the supermarket where he shops had instituted a new discount card program. If you signed up for the free card, you received posted discounts on various products in the store. The first product he bought with his new card was a 1-pound bag of coffee. The coffee, normally priced at $8.25 per pound, sold for $6.60. What percentage of savings did Lin receive?

    _____

Mailing Cost Mysteries

There are many different mailing options for the postal customer. Below are some of the most commonly used mailing options. (Weights and costs may vary.)

First Class Mail: This category is for letters, bills, brochures, and catalogs that weigh 13 ounces (369 g) or less. First class mail is relatively fast and arrives at its destination in the continental U.S. in less than a week.

Parcel Post: This category describes packages that weigh less than 70 pounds (32 kg). The maximum package size allowed is 130 inches (330 cm). This 130-inch limit represents the length of the package plus its girth.

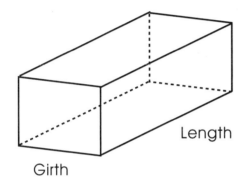

Length

Girth

These parcel requirements can be expressed as a formula.

Length   +   Girth   =   130 inches or less
(Girth is: Width + Width + Height + Height)

So our maximum size formula for a normal parcel may be simplified.
Length + (2W + 2H) = 130 inches or less

Priority Mail: This category includes mail or parcels as described above. It is a faster means of delivery, usually two to three days. It also costs more than first class or parcel post.

Express Mail: This category includes mail or parcels. It is the fastest means of delivery, guaranteed overnight in most places in the continental U.S. It costs much more than priority mail.

Media Mail: Formerly referred to as "book rate," this is a reduced cost method for mailing qualified heavier "media" materials. Media mail is typically not delivered as quickly as first class or priority mail.

Mailing Cost Mysteries (cont.)

Answer the questions below using the mailing options found on page 81.

1. Brad has an envelope to mail. The envelope and its contents weigh 10 ounces (283 g) and could be mailed first class at a cost of $2.23. It costs $3.50 to send an item up to one pound via priority mail. How much more will Brad spend if he decides to go with priority mail rather than first class?

   _____

2. A manufacturer is sending product samples to a customer. The manufacturer cannot change the girth of this product sample as it is a fixed size. The product must be packed in such a way that the width of the box used is 22 inches (55.8 cm) and the height of the box is 30 inches (76 cm). However, the length of the box can be customized to meet postal regulations. What is the maximum length this box could be made and still meet the mailing-size requirement for parcels?

   _____

3. The Spring Season catalogs went out via first class mail early last week at a cost of $2.86 each. Richard has since discovered that he forgot to mail 21 catalogs. He must now choose between priority mail at a cost of $3.50 per catalog or express mail at a cost of $16.00 per catalog. How much more will it cost to send this group of catalogs via express mail instead of priority mail?

   _____

4. Josephine wants to test the value of priority mail against that of express mail by sending two packages of the same size and weight to one of her offices out of state. She has instructed employees to note the exact time of delivery for each package. The priority mail package cost $7.55 to send and it arrived in two days. The express mail package cost $24.50, but arrived in less than one day. After comparing the two, Josephine decided that express mail was not a good business value since the one day made little difference. As a percentage, about how much did it cost to send the priority mail package versus the express mail package?

   _____

Name _____

More Mailing Cost Mysteries

Customers mailing packages may choose to purchase insurance to protect the value of contents against damage or loss. Insurance costs $1.10 for packages valued at $50.00 or less. Packages valued at $50.01 to $100.00 cost $2.00 to insure. Packages valued at $100.01 to $200.00 cost $3.00 to insure. Each increment from this point through $1,000 costs $1.00 more per $100.00 of value to insure.

Use the information regarding postal insurance above and mailing fees on (page 81) to answer questions about the situations below.

1. Brenda is sending four packages via priority mail at a cost of $5.15 each. Each contains an expensive vase valued at $375.00. How much will her total bill for this mailing be if she decides to purchase insurance on each package? _____

2. How much will a postal customer's bill total if he sends a package via express mail at a cost of $18.85 and also want to add $675.00 worth of insurance?

   _____

3. Which is a better deal for the consumer in terms of the percentage cost of insurance as a portion of total item value: the insurance cost of a $32.00 item or the insurance cost of a $158.00 item?

   _____

4. If Henderson Bolt & Bracket is sending a bolt that costs $0.89 to a customer as a warranty replacement, why does it not make sense to insure that bolt?

5. Patsy took a large box to her local post office to mail. The box's dimensions were 24 inches (60.9 cm) by 16 inches (40.6 cm) by 28 inches (71 cm). The clerk told Patsy that the box was too large to mail. What would be a concise and polite way for Patsy to explain that the box's size as it relates to the 130-inch size limit does meet the regulations for mailing?

More Mailing Cost Mysteries (cont.)

6. Base Price Books ships their book orders by mail. Every book is sold at 100% of the listed cover price. Their cost on books is 50% of the listed cover price. Base Price Books charges customers a flat fee of $6.00 per order to cover postage and handling. Sometimes they make money on this flat fee, often not. The manager of Base Price Books is continually evaluating shipping methods and costs.

   A. A book order has just come in for $40.00 in books. The order will total $46.00 once postage and handling is added. If this book order costs $2.65 to send via media mail rate and is insured, how much total profit will Base Price Books make on this order?

   _____

   B. From the standpoint of the customer who ordered the books described in part A, what percent of the total cost of this order represents postage and handling?

   _____

   C. Base Price Books mails 800 orders per year in the $50.00 and under price range. If they stopped insuring orders of less than $50.00 and put the money saved into a fund to use for lost or damaged orders, how much money would be in the fund? (Do not include the amount customers pay for postage and handling.)

   _____

7. A postal inspector was examining insurance claims and noticed that a package valued at $800.00 had only a fee of $7.00 collected by the postal clerk for the insurance coverage.

   A. How much should the insurance have cost for an package valued at $800.00?

   _____

   B. The postal inspector suspects that the insured receipt for this item has been altered to show a higher value than the item was originally insured for. Based on the insurance fee that was collected, what was probably the declared value of this item before the amount was altered?

   _____

   C. After studying the receipt under magnification, the inspector concluded that no alterations had been made. The inspector thought of two possibilities. One was that the postal clerk may have made a mistake and simply undercharged the customer for the insurance. What could the other possibility be?

   _____

Name _____

Timing Is Everything

Solve the time-related problems below by making appropriate conversions.

1. A special glue sets in 190 seconds. How many minutes and seconds does that give the user to work with the glue before it sets?

   _____

2. It takes 74 hours for the pump to empty a tank completely at a factory. How would this be expressed as days and hours?

   _____

3. A movie lasts 136 minutes. How long is the movie in hours and minutes?

   _____

4. Craig worked in the yard for 45 minutes on Monday, 55 minutes on Tuesday, and 35 minutes on Wednesday. He thinks another 30-minute session later in the week will finish the work. Expressed as hours and minutes, how much time has Craig already spent on his yard work?

   _____

5. Kit has an appointment in $1\frac{1}{4}$ hours. How many minutes does that give her before the appointment?

   _____

6. Working together, Josh and Tim can wash and wax a car in 40 minutes. They want to figure an hourly rate for their work based on the time they spend per car. What portion of an hour is 40 minutes?

   _____

7. Kent bills clients for his time at a strict rate of $120.00 per hour. How much would he charge a client for a 50-minute consultation?

   _____

Name _____

Metric Measures

Below are three basic units in the metric system.

The **meter** is the basic unit measure of **length**.
The **liter** is the basic unit measure of liquid **capacity**.
The **gram** is the basic unit measure for **mass**.

The basic unit of meters is frequently seen expressed in terms of kilometers (1000 meters) and, for smaller measure, centimeters ($\frac{1}{100}$ of a meter).

Liters are often seen expressed in terms of milliliters, which are $\frac{1}{1000}$ of a liter.

The basic unit of grams is often seen expressed in terms of kilograms (1000 grams) and, for smaller measure, milligrams ($\frac{1}{1000}$ of a gram).

For each of the situations below, state the most appropriate metric measure.

1. The length of a pencil _____

2. The weight of a medium-sized dog _____

3. The amount a water cooler will hold _____

4. A small dose of cough syrup _____

5. The distance between two cities _____

6. The weight of a letter being sent airmail from a foreign country _____

7. The amount of fuel a car's gas tank will hold _____

8. The weight of a hummingbird _____

9. The height of a small child _____

10. The weight of a block of cheese _____

Name _____

Metric Measures (cont.)

For each of the sentences below, supply the conversion needed to make a true statement.

11. 75 kilometers = _____ meters

12. 500 grams = _____ kilogram

13. 300 meters = _____ kilometer

14. 2,000 milliliters = _____ liter

15. 750 milligrams = _____ gram

16. A 2.6-kilometer hike would be _____ meters.

17. A length of rope 375 centimeters might be more appropriately expressed as _____ meters.

18. A 2-liter quantity of olive oil will be divided equally among 4 friends into _____ milliliter amounts.

19. A large pepperoni sausage 1.2 meters in length will cut into 4 equal pieces of _____ centimeters each.

20. A large block of butter weighing 3,200 grams is _____ kilograms.

21. Twenty pieces of licorice each measuring 20 centimeters would stretch _____ meters if laid end to end.

Short Answer

22. Why do you think the metric system is the preferred measurement system for scientific applications?

Random Events

What does **random** mean in a mathematics context? The term *random* denotes a situation in which some event is not specifically selected but occurs by chance. For an event to be truly random, the outcome must not be controlled by a person or by a predictable pattern of circumstances.

Example: Ronald and Gary are pondering the problems in their lives. Gary does not have a date for the upcoming prom. Out of frustration, he announces he will ask the next girl he sees, regardless of who she is, to the prom. A few minutes later a girl approaches. Even though she is at least nine inches taller than Gary, he rushes to ask her to the prom. She flatly refuses. Has a random event occurred? Yes, it actually has. Since Gary did ask the next girl he saw and did not alter his original criteria, the invitation was offered at random.

For each of the events described, write **R** (random) or **NR** (not random).

_____ 1. A blindfolded person draws ticket stubs to determine the winner of a raffle.

_____ 2. Team captains select team members for a playground sport.

_____ 3. A teacher flips a coin 20 times and records the results.

_____ 4. The votes in a U.S. Presidential Election are counted.

_____ 5. A health inspector arrives unexpectedly at a meat processing plant and pulls samples for testing from the production line.

_____ 6. A person examining coffee at the supermarket suddenly remembers a coffee advertisement and decides to buy that brand.

_____ 7. At the game area of an amusement park, a visitor rolls a wooden ball up a sloped surface and the ball drops into the highest scoring bin.

_____ 8. The spinner of a board game usually seems to stop on the green section.

Probability

A **probability** is the likelihood of an event occurring. Mathematics can be used for precisely describing many kinds of probabilities.

Example 1: A bag contains seven marbles, one of which is green. What is the likelihood that the green marble will be drawn from the bag at random on the first attempt?

Since there is only one green marble in this bag, the probability that it would be drawn at random is 1 in 7, or $\frac{1}{7}$. Since a probability is usually expressed as a number between 0 and 1, this probability could also be written 0.1429.

0 is used to denote a probability that has no chance of occurrence.
1 is used to denote a probability that will certainly occur.

Assume that a light-colored marble was drawn on the first try. That marble was not placed back into the bag. The probability of drawing the green marble on the next try would change to 1 in 6, or 0.1667. This is true because the probability changed to reflect the new circumstances.

Example 2: Teresa packed some candy in a paper sack for eating at the theater. Since it will be dark in the theater, she will not be able to see the contents of the bag. She placed three gumballs and nine chocolates inside the bag. The candies are all shaped the same.

What is the probability she will get a gumball the first time she pulls a piece of candy from the bag?

Of the 12 pieces of candy in the bag, 3 are gumballs. So the probability will be 3 in 12, or 0.25.

Probability (cont.)

What is the probability she will get a piece of chocolate candy the first time she draws one from the bag?

Of the pieces of candy in the bag, 9 are chocolates. So the probability will be 9 in 12, or 0.75.

These kinds of simple-event probabilities can be described by the formula below.

$$P = \frac{S}{N}$$

Where **P** is the probability of the specified event occurring, **S** is the outcome being considered, and **N** is the number of possible outcomes.

Compute the probability for each of the situations below. Express your answer as a decimal number.

_____ 1. What is the probability of getting a problem correct on a test if you guess, and the question is multiple choice with possible answer choices of A, B, C, or D?

_____ 2. A six-sided die is rolled to determine the batting order in a neighborhood baseball game. What is the probability a "4" will be turn up on the first roll?

_____ 3. There were 2,000 raffle tickets sold. What is the probability a person will win the raffle if they bought five tickets?

_____ 4. Ten seniors and 30 juniors were asked to take part in a survey. If the interviewer does not know the class ranking of the students, what is the probability a junior will be selected for the first interview?

_____ 5. An artist has a supply box with 86 tubes of paint. Of this number, there are some duplicates. Three tubes are cobalt blue, six tubes are indigo, and four tubes are Windsor blue. The artist will pull one from the box at random and use it as the background color. What is the probability that indigo will be chosen?

Name _____

More About Probabilities

Compute the probability for each of the events below.

_____ 1. A dog gives birth to a litter of puppies with four males and three females. All of the puppies look alike. A family chooses a female puppy to take home once it has been weaned. The owner places a collar on the puppy to tell it apart from the others. What is the probability that the family will get the chosen puppy if the collar falls off?

_____ 2. A game show host has six envelopes, each containing one of the following: a $100.00 bill, a $50.00 bill, a $20.00 bill, a $10.00 bill, a $5.00 bill, or a $1.00 bill. A contestant is told he may choose one of the envelopes or be given $20.00 outright. What is the probability the contestant will end up with more money if he chooses an envelope?

_____ 3. A museum is selling raffle tickets at a cost of $100.00 each, with the prize being a $30,000 automobile. At the time of the drawing only 91 of the 400 tickets printed have been sold. What is the probability of a person winning the car who has bought only 2 raffle tickets?

Short Answer
Some may involve computing a probability.

4. Why might a life insurance company be more eager to issue a policy for a 30-year-old, married, mother of two who does not smoke than for a 45-year-old male who smokes and has never been married?

5. Suppose the probability that your teacher will give a test next Thursday is 80%. What is the probability that your teacher will not give a test next Thursday?

6. Suppose the national weather bureau says there is a 1 in 3 chance of thunderstorms on Wednesday. It reports a 40% precipitation probability on Thursday. On which day does the weather bureau think precipitation is more likely?

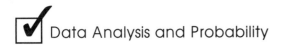

Name _____

Data Analysis

The first female mathematician to appear in historical accounts was Hypatia of Alexandria. About 1,600 years ago, Hypatia became the head of an important school of philosophy and mathematics in Alexandria. It is thought that she was killed because her work was considered pagan. Her death began the beginning of an intolerant era and marked the decline of Alexandria as a center of learning in the ancient world.

About 1,500 years ago, the Roman Emperor, Justinian, closed schools that taught philosophy, science, and mathematics because he considered them pagan. A millennium of learning and accumulated information was set aside. Baghdad then became the unofficial capitol of scientific learning for the next few centuries.

History tells us that the pursuit of knowledge cannot be halted indefinitely. The human mind is curious and knowledge will be pursued, and new information sought. But how is this information or data accumulated and studied? How is data taken in and ultimately made into something useful?

The activities in this section are built around the theme of data accumulation and analysis. The understanding of a body of data and the techniques available for studying such data are essential for many fields of study and occupations.

For Further Research
Computers have revolutionized humankind's ability to process and analyze data. Beginning with America's early space program, what has the development of the computer meant for science, architecture, medicine, or business? Consider these broad aspects of computer application, and then select a more narrowed topic for independent research. For example, you may wish to focus on the role of computers in proving math theorems or the way in which businesses use accumulated data to market products. It may be beneficial to work with a classmate for this project to produce a short presentation for your classmates.

Name _____

Data

Numbers or other pieces of information that are collected and used for study are known as data. The following are some everyday examples of data being collected and used.

- A teacher asks students to write their home telephone numbers and parent contact information on an index card.
- A cancer researcher analyzes patient records as part of a study testing the effectiveness of a new cancer treatment drug.
- A newspaper reporter sorting through automobile accident reports discovers that there are four times as many accidents occurring at a particular intersection than the next most accident-prone site.

For each of the situations described below, write "D" if the item is a form of data or "ND" if the item is not a form of data.

_____ 1. A farmer knows that a pile of rocks is at the edge of a plowed field, but he does not know how many rocks are in the pile.

_____ 2. Fourteen dogs consume four large bags of dog food per week as shown in the kennel's financial records.

_____ 3. Consumers, on average, spent less money on books in 1999 than in 2001.

_____ 4. An evening apartment fire caused 12 families to seek other shelter.

_____ 5. In a survey of the people who tasted a particular new soft drink, 50% did not like the taste.

_____ 6. A walk-in freezer at a meat packing facility has been monitored and will not cool below 27 degrees.

_____ 7. Two people in seven failed the driver's licensing test on the first attempt.

_____ 8. A moving truck is nearly empty except for a small stack of boxes.

Samples and Populations

Data can be collected in a variety of ways. Polling large numbers of people before an election is an example of collecting data. Recording the types and numbers of birds visiting a backyard bird feeder would be another example. Some Web sites, often without people even knowing, gather data about those who visit the sites.

In a general sense, researchers who gather data look at a sample of an overall population. For example, the people who are attending a sporting event at a large stadium might represent a population of sports fans in that area. If you asked ten of the people what type of concession snack they prefer, then those people have become your sample of the much larger stadium population.

Studying a sample enables researchers to make predictions without having to actually study the entire population. Sometimes the predictions made about a population will be wrong because the information gathered was faulty or did not accurately represent the overall population. In spite of the drawbacks, using a sample provides researchers a good opportunity to study a larger population, sometimes with startling accuracy.

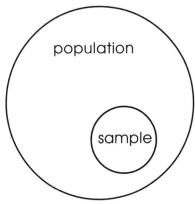

For each of the samples below, write what the larger population would be. There are many possible correct answers.

1. The students enrolled in Mr. Craven's music class at New Briton elementary school

_____

2. People who voted in the last local election

_____

Samples and Populations (cont.)

3. Water samples taken from different locations within a national park _____

   _____

4. The rats living in a condemned building at the corner of 12th Avenue and Main

   Street _____

5. People who belong to a trade union in a particular state _____

   _____

6. Radio listeners who listen to talk radio programs during the daytime _____

   _____

For each of the populations described below, write a smaller sample that could be taken. There will be many possible answers.

7. The members of a local health club _____

8. Scientists who study environmental issues _____

9. All migrating birds _____

10. Animals that live year-round in cold-weather environments _____

11. People who have had a serious illness requiring hospitalization _____

12. Causes of delays in airline travel _____

More About Samples and Populations

Since accurate data can be a valuable resource, it is important to select an appropriate sample before beginning the process of collecting data. For example, you would not ask people in a "no pets allowed" apartment building about their pets' favorite foods. Choosing the right sample is an important step in data gathering.

Short Answer

1. If a sample may not give an accurate picture of a population, why not study the entire population?

2. Why is it important to choose an appropriate sample when collecting data?

3. Do you think that data can be manipulated, based on the way it is collected, in an attempt to prove a particular point of view? Why or why not?

More About Samples and Populations (cont.)

In the situations described below write a check mark on the line to identify the sample you think is most appropriate for the research situation described. Be prepared to discuss the reasons for your choice.

1. The student editor of the school yearbook wants to find out why sales of the yearbook have declined in recent years.
_ Sample only those students who bought the yearbook last year, asking them a series of questions about its design and content.
_ Sample only those students who did not buy the yearbook last year, asking them a series of questions about its design and content.
_ Show the yearbook to people at the mall, asking them a series of questions about its design and content.

2. A bicycle manufacturer wants to choose new colors for a line of rugged mountain bikes marketed to outdoor enthusiasts.
_ Sample the fans at a professional football game, asking them to rank the possible new colors.
_ Sample the participants at a skateboard event, asking them to rank the possible new colors.
_ Sample bicycle shop owners, asking them to rank the possible new colors.

3. A scientist wants to determine the exact types and quantities of food eaten by coyotes.
_ Ask ranchers in the area what coyotes eat.
_ Ask scientists who study other animal populations to relate what they have observed regarding coyotes.
_ Study coyotes in the wilderness, observing them firsthand as much as possible.

4. An environmental group wishes to find out what the average citizen thinks about certain environmental issues.
_ Ask randomly-selected people at an anti-nuclear energy protest if they will take a few minutes to give their opinions on environmental issues.
_ Ask randomly-selected people entering a grocery store if they will take a few minutes to give their opinions on environmental issues.
_ Ask randomly-selected employees from a local factory if they will take a few minutes at the end of their shift to give their opinions on environmental issues.

Collecting Data

Tables and **graphs** are two basic ways of visually displaying data. A simple table or graph allows information to be seen and readily understood, often with just a glance.

Frequency tables are commonly used for organizing information as it is collected. A basic frequency table can use tally marks to denote the data as it is collected. See the example below.

Example: As part of a research project, Dana has been observing customers who enter a local coffee shop. She watched for one hour on a busy morning and created a frequency table.

Coffee House Customers
Tuesday Morning, one-hour time span

Gender	Frequency
Male	‖‖‖‖ ‖‖‖‖ ‖‖‖‖ ‖‖‖‖ │
Female	‖‖‖‖ ‖‖‖‖ ‖‖‖‖ ‖‖‖‖ │││

Dana was careful to label the frequency table with a title, so that its contents could be easily identified. She also employed a good research technique by collecting the data herself, instead of relying on secondhand sources.

This simple table organizes the information and makes it readily available for portraying in a graph. In this example, only the gender of each customer was observed, but a frequency table could also be used where there are many categories to be observed and large numbers of data items to be noted.

Collecting Data (cont.)

Use frequency tables to organize data as it is collected. A general interest magazine will be needed for this activity.

1. Select a popular magazine and use the frequency table below to describe its composition. Study each page of the magazine beginning with the first page, looking for the following categories: **Content, Photographs and Illustrations, Advertisements.** If a page of the magazine is 50% or more devoted to advertising, then place a tally mark on the frequency table next to **Advertisements.** If the page is 50% or more devoted to non-advertisement photographs or illustrations, then place a tally mark next to **Photographs.** If the page is 50% or more related to content, such as text, stories, articles, recipes, etc., then place a tally mark next to **Content.**

Magazine Composition by Page for (title)_____

Page Type   **Frequency**

Content

Photographs

Advertisements

What category was most represented in the magazine you chose? _____

Did the results surprise you? Why or why not? _____

2. Select a single page from the magazine you chose for activity 1. Make certain that it is a Content page with lots of text. Then select six commonly used words and construct a frequency table to identify the number of times those words are used on the page you selected. You will have to read each line of your content page, carefully looking for your selected words.

What type of words appeared to be the most common on the page you selected? _____

Did any commonly used words pop up that surprised you? _____

Organizing Data

Setting an appropriate interval for data is an essential part of being able to portray the data in a meaningful way. An interval that is set too large, or too small, tends to make the data have a lopsided look.

Example: Celia interviewed library patrons about their reading habits. Part of her survey consisted of gathering information about the ages of those library patrons. She interviewed ten people. Their ages are listed below:

12, 19, 20, 20, 22, 24, 28, 35, 48, 51

Her first frequency table displaying the age data looked like the following:

Ages of Library Patrons Interviewed

Interval	Frequency
12 years and under	/
Over 12 years	⊬⊬⊬ ////

The intervals selected for this frequency table do not break the ages down into groups that are small enough to give a good view of the data. Most of the people interviewed were in their 20s, a fact not made clear by the large interval chosen.

Now examine Celia's second frequency table.

Ages of Library Patrons Interviewed

Interval	Frequency
Age 10 to 19	✓✓
Age 20 to 29	✓✓✓✓
Age 30 and older	✓✓✓

While this table contains the same data, it better portrays the data by using smaller intervals. In this table it is clear that more of those interviewed were in their 20s. This frequency table would also allow the data to be depicted on a graph in a more meaningful way.

Organizing Data (cont.)

For the data given below, select an appropriate interval and fill in the frequency tables with tally marks to accurately portray the data. Depending on the intervals you select, some of the spaces on the frequency tables may not be used.

1. A group of test scores from a social studies class: 75, 55, 45, 80, 90, 100, 40, 75, 70, 85, 60, 95, 100, 95, 95, 90, 60, 80, 70, 65, 85, 100, 90, 85, 95, 20, 100, 75.

Social Studies Class Test Scores

Interval   Frequency

_____   _____

_____   _____

_____   _____

_____   _____

_____   _____

_____   _____

_____   _____

_____   _____

_____   _____

2. Purchases made from the petty cash fund of Oak Avenue Hardware Store during the month of October: $1.89, $2.12, $4.84, $3.06, $0.98, $6.55, $12.45, $3.69, $1.88, $5.05, $7.49, $0.78, $8.31, $8.12, $16.55, $2.37, $4.99, $0.45.

October Petty Cash Expenditures, Oak Ave. Hardware

Interval   Frequency

_____   _____

_____   _____

_____   _____

_____   _____

_____   _____

_____   _____

_____   _____

_____   _____

_____   _____

_____   _____

Analyzing Data

Measures of central tendency provide a means for both summarizing and describing the data in a mathematical way.

The **median, mode,** and **mean** are three methods used in analyzing data. Each provides a different kind of look at the data being studied.

Median

The median is, perhaps, the easiest of the three to determine. In an ordered set of data (a set where the number values have been listed from least to greatest), the median is simply the middle-most data value. In a set with an even amount of members, the median is the average of the two center numbers.

Example: For the following set of data: < 1, 5, 7, 12, 22 >, 7 is the median of this set. Counting from either direction towards the center will show that 7 is clearly the middle value of this set.

Mode

The mode refers to the member of the data set that most often occurs. Once a data set has been ordered, it is much easier to tell which member of the set is the mode. Some data sets will have no mode, as no numbers are repeated within that set. Other data sets may have several modes, if different members of the data set have the same number of occurrences. Check the examples below.

Example 1: < 1, 2, 17, 34, 122, 3018, 4667 > No mode is present in this set.

Example 2: < 9, 9, 11, 12, 13, 13, 13 > The mode of this set is 13.

Example 3: < 2, 2, 2, 4, 4, 6, 6, 6, 16 > The modes of this set are 2 and 6.

Name _____

Analyzing Data (cont.)

For each of the data sets below, determine the **median** and the **mode**. Some of the data sets may have no mode or more than one. Be sure to order the data before beginning each problem.

1. < 201, 222, 212, 211, 201, 800, 1,200, 222, 208, 208, 201, 224, 248 >

    median_____ mode_____

2. < 16, 14, 12, 10, 8, 4, 4, 2, 2 >

    median_____ mode_____

3. < 9, 13, 7, 21 >

    median_____ mode_____

4. < 112, 1064, 373 >

    median_____ mode_____

5. < 1, 1, 3, 2, 4, 3, 4, 2, 2, 1, 3, 4, 5, 7, 4, 3, 2, 1, 3, 5 >

    median_____ mode_____

6. < 44, 88 >

    median_____ mode_____

7. < 45, 55, 75, 45, 55, 75, 45, 55, 95, 45, 65, 75, 85 >

    median_____ mode_____

8. < 24, 26, 12, 24, 16, 4, 4, 0, 0, 12, 24, 16, 12, 8 >

    median_____ mode_____

More About Analyzing Data

Mean
Commonly called the average, the mean is obtained by adding all the members of the data set together, then dividing that sum by the total number of members in the data set.

Example: For the set < 4, 14, 18, 18, 28, 40, 88 > , the average is found by:

Step 1   4 + 14 + 18 + 18 + 28 + 40 + 88 = 210

Step 2   210 ÷ 7 = **30**

The mean of this set is 30.

Determine the **mean** for each of the data sets below.

1. < 33, 99, 99 >

    mean _____

2. < 100, 200, 300, 500, 1,000, 1,200, 1,400, 1,700 >

    mean _____

3. < 12, 12, 20, 21, 10, 14, 16 >

    mean _____

4. < 64, 74, 78, 79, 84, 89, 90, 97, 99, 102, 108, 110, 124 >

    mean _____

5. < 1, 2, 2, 2, 3, 3, 4, 5, 5 >

    mean _____

6. < 110, 125, 155, 255, 225, 235, 185, 190, 195, 345 >

    mean _____

More About Analyzing Data (cont.)

We have seen that the **mean, median,** and **mode** all provide different views of a data set. But why bother with all three? Why not just select one of the measures of central tendency and use it as the standard all of the time? The answer is best shown with examples.

Example: If there are only five houses on Elm Street, which of the measures would give the best picture of a typical house on this particular street?

The appraised values of each of the houses are:

$80,000 $88,000 $94,000 $98,000 $288,000

The **mean** price of the houses on this street is $129,600. But four of the five houses on this street are far more modest in value. The single house with a very high value has driven the average up beyond the point where it accurately portrays the data set.

There is no **mode**, so that measure is useless for this data set.

The **median** price of houses on this street is $94,000. This figure more closely represents the values of the houses on this street. In fact it is quite common for housing prices in a region to be listed in terms of the median price.

You can see from this example that a particular measure may not be suitable for using with a particular data set, since it may not yield an accurate picture of the data.

Determine whether the **mean** or the **median** would provide the best measure for the data set described. Note: The mode will not be used with this exercise since the actual data sets are not provided.

_____ 1. The science test results of a small class of six students where all scores were passing except for one very low failing score

_____ 2. The wages and salaries of all employees at a very large corporation

_____ 3. The number of miles a car consistently runs on a given amount of fuel

_____ 4. The eggs produced by chickens at a large egg farm

Using Data to Make Predictions

Interpolation and **extrapolation** are two basic techniques for analyzing data. Both techniques involve using known data to make predictions about the unknown.

Interpolation is the process of making a prediction between known data points.

Extrapolation is the process of making a prediction beyond a known data point.

Example: The Art Function Glass Company is a growing business that specializes in making decorative glass items, window panes, and other functional glass products. The company's sales figures are shown on the graph below. One year's sales figures were not available to be shown on the graph.

The Art Function Glass Company Sales 1989 – 1997

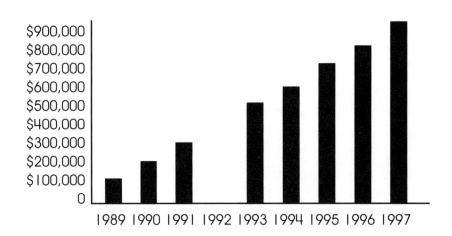

1989	$100,000	1990	$200,000	1991	$300,000
1992		1993	$500,000	1994	$600,000
1995	$700,000	1996	$800,000	1997	$900,000

Using Interpolation: What were sales for this company in 1992?
Since there are several years of steadily increasing sales figures prior to 1992, and several more years beyond 1992, a pattern has been revealed by the known data. A likely figure for 1992's sales would be $400,000. However, since the actual 1992 sales figures are not known, the figure of $400,000 cannot be stated with certainty. It is only a prediction that is based on what can be observed in the known data set.

Name _____

Using Data to Make Predictions (cont.)

Using Extrapolation: How much were sales for this company in 1998?
Sales must have been $1,000,000 in 1998. Well not exactly. While the known sales figures for this company do show a steadily increasing trend, it can only be predicted that sales were $1,000,000 in 1998. However, since that information is not shown, it cannot be assumed. 1998 could have been the year that this company tripled sales from previous year. 1998 might also have been the year that a fire destroyed the factory, thus reducing the profits.

For each of the situations described below, write **interpolation** or **extrapolation** in the blank to denote which technique is being described.

_____ 1. A business person is trying to predict the new values of properties near a planned amusement park.

_____ 2. A stock trader uses prices of stocks over a three-month period to predict tomorrow's closing price of a stock.

_____ 3. A researcher makes an important discovery in the laboratory and tries to recreate the experiment by repeating the conditions that led to the discovery.

_____ 4. A farmer looks at rainfall data collected over many years and tries to predict how much rain will fall during the upcoming growing season.

_____ 5. A researcher tries to determine the past population growth of a historical city over a period of years for which there is only sporadic data available.

_____ 6. A wildlife biologist tries to predict the future rate of decline of an animal population based on past and current observations.

_____ 7. A person, who knows the precise sunrise time for both Monday and Wednesday, is trying to calculate Tuesday's sunrise time.

_____ 8. A member of the track team has been charting the practice times of team members over a period of weeks, carefully noting their improvement in hopes of predicting their performance at an upcoming track meet.

More About Using Data To Make Predictions

Use the data shown below to answer questions, making predictions based on the techniques of interpolation and extrapolation. You may first want to organize the data into a table or graph on a separate sheet of paper.

A biologist has been studying the population of trout for several years at a remote lake in the Northwest. The study was begun in 1994. Her data is shown below.

| 1994—720 | 1995—810 | 1997—800 | 1998—710 |
| 1999—630 | 2000—520 | | |

1. In 1996, funding was not available to carry out the study, so no data was collected at the lake. What figure might be predicted for the lake's trout population during 1996?

2. What prediction might the biologist make about the lake's population before the data is collected for the year 2001? What risk is associated with making this kind of prediction?

3. Describe the situation with the trout population at this lake and the trend that appears to be developing regarding the population.

Short Answer

4. Between interpolation and extrapolation, which method would you defend as being more accurate for making predictions? Why?

5. What is the main problem posed by using either interpolation or extrapolation, especially if the results are important?

               IF87128 *Standards-Based Math*

More Work with Data

Take the list of steps shown below and rewrite them in the proper order for conducting a research project that involves data.

A. The data is analyzed to determine its possible meaning(s).
B. Data is collected for the research project.
C. An appropriate sample is selected from the population being studied.
D. The data may then be used for making decisions or predictions.
E. A topic for research is decided upon.
F. Data is organized in a way that is useful.

1. _____
2. _____
3. _____
4. _____
5. _____
6. _____

True or False

_____ 7. The term *average* is a synonym for median.
_____ 8. Data can be nearly any kind of information that has been collected.
_____ 9. A sample will always be a subset of a larger population.
_____ 10. One of the uses of a frequency table is for tallying information as it is collected.
_____ 11. Graphs give a visual format of data that is usually more confusing than a text explanation of the data.
_____ 12. The mean is always a better measure for data sets than the median.

Determine the mean, median, and mode for the data sets shown below.
13. < 28, 18, 88, 112, 84, 64, 121, 28, 12, 18, 62, 22, 28 >

mean _____   median _____   mode _____

14. < 170, 320, 200 >

mean _____   median _____   mode _____

15. < 2,000 , 200 , 20,000 , 200,000 , 20 >

mean _____   median _____   mode _____

Name _____

More Work with Data (cont.)

Every year, Rita goes to Lake James to stay for her summer vacation. Six years ago she began taking a reading of the lake's water level on the last day of her vacation. She measures the level according to a mark she made on one of the posts of her dock, the baseline against which all other measures are taken. Here are her figures, as recorded in a section of her journal.

Year 1: Average rainfall, marked post to denote baseline water level.
Year 2: Average rainfall, water level is still 1.5 inches below mark on post.
Year 3: Lots of rain this summer, water level is only 1 inch above mark.
Year 4: Average rainfall, but water level is 2.5 inches below mark.
Year 5: -- forgot to make entry
Year 6: Average rainfall, but water level continues to fall, now at 6 inches below mark!
Year 7: Lots of rain this summer, but water level is still 5 inches below mark?

16. From looking at Rita's journal, what sort of trend do you think she believes is occurring at the lake? (You may want to organize this data on a bar graph to help with your analysis.)

17. What probably happened with the lake's level during year 5 when the entry was omitted? Can it be determined with certainty?

Short Answer

18. What effect would data that is collected for a research project have on the project if it were later determined that the sample used was not representative of the population being studied?

19. Why is organizing data such an important part of the overall task of collecting and analyzing data?

20. Explain how different measures of central tendency can give different views of a data set.

Comprehensive Practice

Mixed Review

Solve.

1. What is the decimal equivalent of the fraction $\frac{1}{12}$? _____

2. How much would the sales tax be on a purchase of $84.00 in an area where the sales tax rate is 5.5%? _____

3. How much money in simple interest would a savings account with an annual interest rate of $6\frac{1}{4}$% and a beginning balance of $1,200 earn in one year?
   _____

4. What would be the next number in this pattern if it is described by $x + 4$?
   28, _____

5. List all factors of 40. _____

6. Is 63 a prime number? _____

7. Is 40 a multiple of 60? _____

8. What is the greatest common factor of $24y$ and $48y$? _____

9. What would be the least common denominator for $\frac{2}{3}$ and $\frac{1}{9}$? _____

10. Solve $1\frac{5}{8} + 2\frac{1}{12}$ = _____

11. Solve $\frac{1}{2}$ divided by $\frac{3}{4}$ = _____

12. A ratio of 5:12 exists between art majors and history majors at a local college. If there are 60 history majors at this college, then how many art majors are there?
    _____

13. How many sides are present on a square-based pyramid? _____

14. What is the perimeter of a hexagon with sides of $2\frac{2}{3}$ cm? _____

15. What is the area of a circle with radius of 11 feet, 6 inches? _____

Comprehensive Practice (cont.)

16. What is the surface area of a cube with sides of 3.5 cm? _____

17. Do the sides 10, 24, 26 describe a right triangle? _____

18. In what quadrant would the following point lie in a coordinate plane? (3, –3)
    _____

19. If a van was driven 201 miles on $16\frac{1}{4}$ gallons of fuel, what was its miles per gallon rating for this trip? _____

20. How much would $4\frac{3}{4}$ pounds of lobster cost a person if the price per pound is $11.99? _____

21. A lengthy movie of 145 minutes could also be expressed as _____ hrs. _____ min.

22. Would the frogs used in a particular laboratory experiment more likely represent a sample of all frogs or a population of all frogs? _____

Short Answer

23. Why is it important to choose an appropriate sample when collecting data for study?

24. Why might a scientist be reluctant to use data for a study which she has not collected herself?

25. Why are different statistical measures such as mean, median, and mode so commonly used when using just a single measure might be easier to track?

Comprehensive Practice (cont.)

26. If an auction house charges a 12.5% commission on the sale of art items, how much would the commission be on a painting that sold at auction for 1.2 million dollars? _____

27. Dora invested $250.00 in an idea which she later discovered was a pyramid scheme. The person who lured Dora into the scheme gave her $50.00 of her money back before the pyramid scheme collapsed. As a percentage of her original $250.00 investment, how much did Dora lose? _____

28. What would be the next number in the following number pattern? 67, 69, 72, 74, 77, 79, 82, _____

29. In the following function, $y = 7x$, what is the value of y when $x = \frac{2}{3}$? _____

30. In the following function $f(x) = 40 - x$, what is the value of the function when $x = -120$? _____

31. List all factors of 29. _____

32. Is 140 a multiple of 35? _____

33. A ratio of 12:24 describes a particular set of gears. What is the simplest way in which this ratio could be written? _____

34. If a rectangle is divided by a line segment drawn to opposite diagonal vertices, what figures are created by the diagonal? _____

Name _____

Comprehensive Practice (cont.)

Short Answer

35. Why would being able to recognize whether a figure will tessellate be of importance to someone planning a tiling project with unusual tile shapes?

36. Why is the Pythagorean Theorem of somewhat limited use when considered in the narrow context of all triangles?

37. In a pyramid scheme, why do the people who have gotten into the scheme early have an advantage in terms of getting their money back over those who have entered later?

38. Explain why is it useful to be able to recognize common prime numbers, especially those less than 100.

Name _____

Comprehensive Evaluation

Solve.

1. If the commission rate is 4%, how much would a salesperson earn on the sale of a $2,400 item? _____

2. What is the total cost basis for a stock purchase of 200 shares at $27.25 per share with a commission paid of $89.00? _____

3. What is the missing number in this pattern? 8, 13, 17, _____, 26, 31, 35, …
   _____

4. Is the ordered pair (2, 4) one of the solution points in the function $y = 2x + 2$?
   _____

5. List all factors of 59. _____

6. What is the greatest common factor of 30 and 72? _____

7. Is $30kx$ a multiple of $7k$? _____

8. $1\frac{3}{5}$ divided by 3 = _____

9. In a recent election, 55% of the people casting ballots voted for the Know-Nothing Party while 40% voted for the Know-Everything Party. Express as a simplified ratio the number of Know-Nothing Party votes cast to the number of Know-Everything Party votes cast. _____

10. If a square prism is cut from one vertex to an opposite diagonal vertex with a plane, name the resulting two figures that are produced. _____

11. A rectangle with an area of 240 square inches has one side of 12 inches. What is the length of the other side? _____

12. Compute the area of a triangle with a base of 14 inches and a height of 4 inches. _____

13. What is the length of the hypotenuse of a right triangle with legs of 12 cm and 24 cm? _____

14. Could a line be drawn in such a way that would connect the following two points plotted on a coordinate plane? (2,0) (0,2) _____

Comprehensive Evaluation (cont.)

15. Does the function $y = 3x - 4$ describe a line if solution points were plotted on a coordinate plane? _____

16. Express 0.6 hour as an equivalent number of minutes. _____

17. To how many kilometers does 4,500 meters convert? _____

18. Is a coin being flipped until "heads" is obtained a random event? _____

19. If 200 tickets have been sold for a prize drawing and the ticket stubs placed into a large bowl, what is the probability that a person who purchased 2 tickets will win the prize? _____

20. Compute the mean of the following set of numbers. (28, 12, 64, 88, 14) _____

21. What is the median for the group of numbers in problem 20? _____

22. Does interpolation involve making a prediction beyond the known data?
_____

Short Answer
23. What is the underlying reason that pyramid financial schemes are considered fraudulent in nature?

24. Explain the basic concept behind a line of symmetry.

25. If you were making an important decision based on data, what would be the most important question to ask about the data you are using?

Comprehensive Evaluation (cont.)

26. John has two bathrooms in his house. One bathroom has an older-model toilet that uses 2.5 gallons of water per flush. The newer bathroom has a toilet that uses 1.6 gallons of water per flush. John estimates that each of the bathroom toilets is flushed 24 times per day. If John's estimate is correct, how much less water does the newer toilet use than the old toilet per day? _____

27. Which basic unit of metric measure would be most appropriate for expressing the approximate length of a pencil? _____

28. If the probability of a particular event occurring is 0.25, how would that be expressed as a simplified ratio? _____

29. What is the least common multiple of 40 and 60? _____

30. In the following function $y = -4x$, what is the value of y when $x = \frac{1}{4}$? _____

31. In the following function $f(x) = 24 - 2x$, what is the value of the function when $x = 24$? _____

32. What would be the next member in the following pattern? 2, 7, 6, 11, 10, 15, 14, _____

33. What is the total amount of money Charles would have in his saving account at the end of one year if he deposited $4,000 at an annual interest rate of 6.75% and left the money undisturbed for the entire year? _____

34. If a five-part lecture series featured 70-minute segments, how much total time expressed as hours and minutes was the series? _____ hrs. _____ min.

Short Answer
35. How do currency exchange booths, such as those at airports or banks, make money by exchanging currencies?

Comprehensive Evaluation (cont.)

36. What is the basic difference between two-dimensional and three-dimensional figures?

37. Why are tables, charts, and graphs useful for working with data?

38. In a very general sense, why might interpolation be more likely to yield accurate predictions than extrapolation?

39. From a research standpoint, why is it important to choose a sample that is appropriate in regard to the population being studied?

Answer Key

Money Matters 8
Answers will vary.

Percentages 9
1. 0.98, 490
2. 0.80, 4
3. 0.065, 780
4. 0.008, 0.96
5. 0.01, 0.24
6. 1.50, 45
7. 0.022, 1.056
8. 0.75, 18,750
9. 0.086, 1.3975
10. 0.12, 0.252

1. 0.1429, 14.29%
2. 0.80, 80%
3. 2.625, 262.5%
4. $\frac{1}{2}$, 50%
5. $\frac{3}{4}$, 75%
6. $\frac{1}{5}$, 20%
7. $\frac{1}{1}$, 100%
8. $\frac{9}{10}$, 0.90
9. $\frac{3}{5}$, 0.60
10. $\frac{2}{3}$, 0.6667
11. 0.2222, 22.22%
12. 4.25, 425%

Sales Tax 11
1. $33.44
2. $0.19
3. $150
4. $2.38
5. $8.04
6. $0.04
7. $50
8. $4,125
9. $0.77
10. $0.75
11. It may slow consumer spending when the tax is first implemented, or increased from a current level. Sales taxes probably have little effect on consumer spending thereafter. Some consumers may try to avoid a sales tax by buying mail order, or purchasing items in a state with a smaller sales tax rate.
12. No doubt the state with a higher sales tax will lose some tax revenue to the state with a lower sales tax as consumers go there to make purchases, especially on larger price items.
13. First find 10% of the figure, easily done by inspection. Then take half of that amount.
14. $46.71
15. $2,835
16. $0.13
17. $1.06

Commissions 13
1. $5.89
2. $20,100
3. $14.80
4. $3,000
5. $119.76
6. $2,544.90
7. $7,400
8. $45.68
9. The perception would be that they must push sales much harder, or they stand to earn less money.
10. This practice would tend to make salespeople less aggressive and more relaxed with customers, since their job performance and pay would not be tied so closely to only a sales figure.

**Building a Pyramid the
Old-Fashioned Way** 16
1. A) $700
   B) $2,520
   C) $15,120
   D) $30,100

Interest 18
1. $750
2. $48.40
3. $479.80
4. $20,300
5. Yes

Credit Card Buying 19
1. $35.61
2. $1842.23
3. $7682.85
4. $4,000
5. 8%

Currency Exchange 21
Answers will vary.

Auctions 22
1. $590.40
2. $267.60
3. Heavy Gavel is cheaper by $250.00.
4. $10.20
5. $37.00
6. As the sale price climbs during an auction, the commission rate would begin to take a deeper cut from the sales price.

Stocks 25
1. $3,904.00
2. $17,851.00
3. $2,124.90
4. $44.67

Stock Sales 26
1. $840.25
2. $7,000
3. $1617.10
4. $46,995
5. $19.36
6. $47.70

Answer Key

More Work with Financial Math 28
1. $925.29   **2.** $240   **3.** $ 4,000,000
4. In the case of a bank, the interest paid out on savings is smaller than the interest charged on loans. Therefore, the bank is able to meet all of its financial obligations and to make a profit.

Number Patterns 29
Answers will vary.

Patterns 31
1. 27, 44 Pattern: $y + 5$, $y + 7$
2. 200, 220, 240 Pattern: $y + 20$
3. 106 Pattern: $y \div 2$, $y + 28$
4. 6561 Pattern: y^2
5. 625, 3125 Pattern: $5y$
6. 9, 15, 22 Pattern: It is an addition pattern with an increase of 1 to the increase at each interval.
7. O, L Pattern: The pattern is the alphabet in reverse, with every third letter selected.
8. Pattern: The pattern is 2 triangles followed by 2 squares. The shapes repeat with every 3rd one shaded.

More About Patterns 32
1. The Fibonacci sequence missing members: 8, 13, 21, 34, 55 and 233, 377
2. The Fibonacci variation (2nd series shown) missing members: 7, 11, 18, 29 and 123, 199.
3. Activity: Answers will vary, but many of the ratios produced seem to converge to a value of 0.618034, a figure associated with certain ancient developments, including angle workings of certain geometric figures and such architectural buildings as the Great Pyramid.

Decimation 33
1. 4
2. It is a decimation system in the sense that it prevents a portion of cars from filling tanks on a particular day. The pattern rotates, allowing car tanks to be filled on an alternating basis.

Functions 34
1. A. 9 B. 15   **2.** A. −1 B. 2
3. A. 2 B.$\frac{1}{2}$ **4.** A. $\frac{3}{2}$ or $1\frac{1}{2}$ B. −6
5. A. 4 B. 16

Summation 35
1. 136   **2.** 300   **3.** 5,050
4. 496   **5.** 500,500

Tessellations 36
Answers will vary. The purpose of this activity is not to induce students to memorize rules regarding which figures will tessellate, but to experiment with geometric shapes and their relationships to one another.

Parts and Wholes 37
Answers will vary.

Composite and Prime Numbers 39
1. 1, 2, 4, 5, 10, 20
2. 1, 3, 13, 39
3. 1, 2, 3, 4, 5, 6, 8, 10, 12, 15, 20, 24, 30, 40, 60, 120
4. Prime
5. Prime
6. 1, 2, 4, 8, 16, 32, 64
7. 1, 3, 5, 15, 25, 75
8. 1, 2, 3, 4, 6, 8, 12, 16, 24, 48
9. 1, 2, 3, 4, 5, 6, 10, 12, 15, 20, 30, 60
10. Prime
11. Prime
12. 1, 2, 4, 5, 8, 10, 20, 25, 40, 50, 100, 200

Answer Key

Greatest Common Factors 40

1. 28: 1, 2, 4, 7, 14, 28   35: 1, 5, 7, 35 GCF: 7
2. 24: 1, 2, 3, 4, 6, 8, 12, 24   30:1, 2, 3, 5, 6, 10, 15, 30   GCF: 6
3. 45: 1, 3, 5, 9, 15, 45   60: 1, 2, 3, 4, 5, 6, 10, 12, 15, 20, 30, 60   GCF: 15
4. 16: 1, 2, 4, 8, 16   48: 1, 2, 3, 4, 6, 8, 12, 16, 24, 48   72: 1, 2, 3, 4, 6, 8, 9, 12, 18, 24, 36, 72   GCF: 8
5. 120: 1, 2, 3, 4, 5, 6, 8, 10, 12, 15, 20, 24, 30, 40, 60, 120   160: 1, 2, 4, 5, 8, 10, 16, 20, 32, 40, 80, 160   200: 1, 2, 4, 5, 8, 10, 20, 25, 40, 50, 100, 200   GCF: 40
6. 30: 1, 2, 3, 5, 6, 10, 15, 30   45: 1, 3, 5, 9, 15, 45   90: 1, 2, 3, 5, 6, 9, 10, 15, 18, 30, 45, 90   GCF: 15

Multiples 41

1. 40 **2.** 24 **3.** 42 **4.** 60
5. 84 **6.** 30 **7.** 120 **8.** 240

More About GCF and LCM 42

1. $45y$: y, 1, 3, 5, 9, 15, 45 $60y$: y, 1, 2, 3, 4, 5, 6, 10, 12, 15, 20, 30, 60   GCF: $15y$
2. $16r$: r, 1, 2, 4, 8, 16 $128r$: r, 1, 2, 4, 8, 16, 32, 64, 128   GCF: $16r$
3. 11:1, 11 $33k$: k, 1, 3, 11, 33 $66k^2$: k, k, 1, 2, 3, 6, 11, 22, 33, 66   GCF: $11k$
4. $4r$: r, 1, 2, 4 $7kr$: k, r, 1, 7 $17krt$: k, r, t, 1, 17   GCF: r
5. $24y$ **6.** $20rt$ **7.** $100y^2$

Fractions: A Basic Part of the
Math Process 43

1. 84 **2.** 16 **3.** 48 **4.** 40
5. 6 **6.** 40 **7.** 45 **8.** 93
9. 126 **10.** 410 **11.** $\frac{3}{8}$ **12.** $1\frac{4}{15}$
13. $\frac{10}{21}$ **14.** $3\frac{19}{56}$ **15.** $21\frac{2}{21}$ **16.** $\frac{1}{2}$
17. $\frac{11}{60}$ **18.** $\frac{4}{9}$ **19.** $\frac{25}{56}$ **20.** $1\frac{5}{8}$
21. .875 **22.** 0.6 **23.** 0.0667 **24.** 2.5
25. 3.2308 **26.** 126 sq. ft. **27.** 76.62%

Ratio 44

1. 4 **2.** 48 **3.** 9 **4.** 120
5. 120 **6.** 3 **7.** 4 : 1 **8.** 9,000
9. 4 **10.** 3 **11.** 24 in. by 16 in.

The Elusive and Mysterious
Prime Number 46

1. Larger numbers have more opportunities to be factored, simply due to their size.
2. Answers will vary. Since new large primes are being discovered, who knows when the next will be? It is an ancient problem. Nearly 2,000 years ago, Euclid forwarded an argument for primes similar to the one stated for integers in the problem introduction.
3. Primes over 2 are all odd numbers, but this appears to be their only similarity. Primes do not follow a known pattern and therefore no formula has been developed to reveal primes reliably.

Geometry 47

Answers will vary.

The Earth Is Flat 49

Answers will vary for this section. Some suggestions:

1. Dr. Seuss's *The Lorax* weaves an environmental message within the story.
2. Geometric figures are easily classified at a glance, making them a good choice for a book critical of class systems.

Geometric Figures—
A Different Perspective 50

Drawings and captions will vary.

Answer Key

More About Perspective 52

1.

2.

3.

4.

5.

6.

Wrap It Up, and I'll Take It 54

1.

2.

3.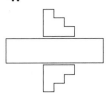

4.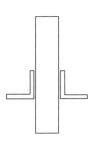

5.

6.

Knowing Your Way Around 56

1. 76 cm   **2.** 22.5 or $22\frac{1}{2}$ in.

3. 188.496 m   **4.** 362 ft.   **5.** 17.5 in.

6. 39.8039 ft. or nearly 39 ft, $9\frac{1}{2}$ in.

7. 42 ft.   **8.** 31.415 ft.

Open Spaces 57

1. 800 sq. in.   **2.** 49 sq. in.

3. 10.9375 sq. in.

4. 113.097 sq. m   **5.** 227.7265 sq. in.

6. 63.75 sq. in.   **7.** 125 sq. ft.

8. 40,920 sq. ft.

9. A. 4,320 sq. ft.   B. 0.8333%

10. 2,551.6833 sq. ft.   **11.** A. $ 3.67

More About Area 59

1.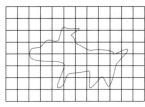

2.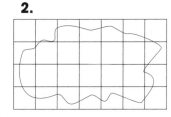

3. Smaller grids lend more precision and are therefore more likely to yield a better estimate.

4. The shape of the figure would be an important factor. The way the pieces are counted toward accumulating the wholes would also be important.

Inside Out 61

1. 108 cubic cm   **2.** 72 cubic in.

3. 3141.5 cubic cm   **4.** 804.169 cubic cm

5. 768 cubic ft.   **6.** $V = q^3$

7. $V = \frac{1}{3}y^2 h$ **8.** $V = \pi r^3$

9. $V = (\pi r^2 h) - (\frac{1}{3}\pi r^2 h)$ **10.** 1,600 cubic in.

11. A. rectangular, by 5,530.7 cubic in.

12. 1,402.5 cubic in.

           IF87128 *Standards-Based Math*

Answer Key

Surface Area..**63**

  1. 3,168 sq. in.

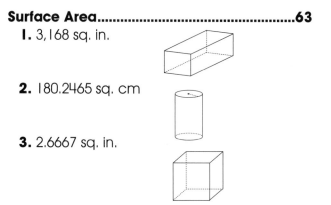

  2. 180.2465 sq. cm

  3. 2.6667 sq. in.

The Pythagorean Theorem **65**

  1. Yes   **2.** Yes   **3.** Yes   **4.** Yes
  5. No   **6.** No   **7.** Yes   **8.** No
  9. 10.7703 ft.   **10.** 5 ft.   **11.** 50 miles
  12. 60 inches
  13. It only works for right triangles.

**More About the
Pythagorean Theorem** **66**
Answers will vary.

More Work with Geometry **67**

  1. 0.1194 mile (nearly $\frac{1}{8}$ of a mile)
  2. A. 2506 sq. cm.   B. larger
  3. A. No   B. 2548.38 cubic in.
  4. A. 7 panels   B. 4 panels
  5. Yes, a right triangle can be made from
      almost any 3 boards, but overlap or waste
      may occur in some combinations. Using
      these three boards, the maximum
      hypotenuse would be 7.8102 ft.

Coordinate Plane Graphing..........................**68**

  1. (5, 3)   **2.** (9, 3)   **3.** (1, 4)   **4.** (0, 3)
  5. L   **6.** C   **7.** F   **8.** J
  9. 12 square units   **10.** 6 square units
  11. 5 units   **12.** (5, 2)   **13.** H, E   **14.** B, C, J
  15. No, the points appear scattered and
      unrelated.
  16. Probably not beyond the general
      conclusion that some of the people of this
      neighborhood have bought products in
      the past. The points do not appear to
      represent a particular pattern or
      concentration.
  17. In this new context, the information takes
      on a different light. A pattern of robberies
      has occurred in this neighborhood
      specifically involving convenience stores.
      An astute detective would want to pay
      close attention to the fact that a single
      store has not yet been robbed.

          IF87128 *Standards-Based Math*

Answer Key

More About Coordinate Plane Graphing 70

1. IV **2.** I **3.** III **4.** IV
5. II **6.** II **7.** III **8.** II
9.

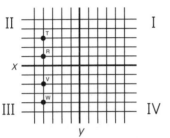

10. Yes, the equation is $x = -4$
11. (1, 3), (2, 5), (−1, −1), (−2, −3)

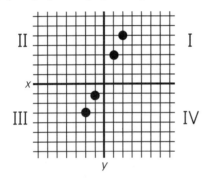

12. (0, −3), (−1, −8), (−2, −13), (1, 2), (2, 7), (3, 12)

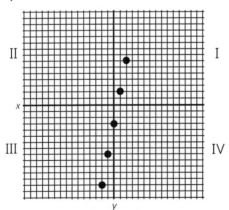

13. (0, 1) **14.** (0, −3)

Lines of Symmetry 73

1. Yes **2.** No **3.** No **4.** No
5. Yes **6.** Yes **7.** No **8.** Yes

Rotation Around an Axis 74

1. **2.**

3. **4.**

The Famous Map Coloring Problem 75

Answers will vary for exercises **1–3.**
4. Sometimes the number of regions present, and the place where the coloring is started, can affect how few colors are used. The process can be compared to the strategy involved in some board games.

Practical Matters 77

Answers will vary.

Miles Per Gallon 78

1. 54.2857 **2.** 14.784 **3.** 35.4167
4. $82.06 **5.** 14.4
6. $0.16, almost $16\frac{1}{2}$ cents **7.** $822.93
8. 80 min. or 1 hr., 20 min.
9. Answers will vary since many factors influence fuel economy. Some are: engine efficiency, maintenance habits, quality of fuel used, and vehicle loads.

Math in Aisle 5—Cleanup at the Register 80

1. 17 cans **2.** $0.67 **3.** $0.01 **4.** 20%

Mailing Cost Mysteries 82

1. $1.27 **2.** 26 inches **3.** $262.50
4. Just a bit over 30%, Priority costs about $\frac{1}{3}$ of express mail in this case.

 IF87128 *Standards-Based Math*

Answer Key

More Mailing Cost Mysteries 83
- **1.** $40.60   **2.** $26.85
- **3.** Insuring the $158.00 item is cheaper as a percentage cost.
- **4.** The cost of the item is less than the insurance would have been for it.
- **5.** My understanding of the postal regulation is that a box of combined size up to 130 inches is allowed. This one is acceptable since its length plus girth measurement is only 112 inches.
- **6.** A. $22.25   B. 13%   C. $880
- **7.** A. $9   B. $600   C. A possibility would be the clerk charged the customer for $800.00 of insurance coverage, prepared the receipt for less, and pocketed the difference.

Timing Is Everything 85
- **1.** 3 min., 10 sec.   **2.** 3 days, 2 hrs.
- **3.** 2 hrs., 16 min.   **4.** 2 hrs., 15 min.
- **5.** 75 min.   **6.** $\frac{2}{3}$ or 0.6667
- **7.** $100.00

Metric Measures 86
- **1.** cm   **2.** kg   **3.** liters   **4.** mL
- **5.** km   **6.** g   **7.** liters   **8.** mg
- **9.** cm   **10.** g or kg   **11.** 75,000
- **12.** 0.5   **13.** 0.3   **14.** 2   **15.** 0.75
- **16.** 2,600   **17.** 3.75   **18.** 500   **19.** 300
- **20.** 3.2   **21.** 4
- **22.** The metric system is precise, and the conversions are based on units of ten. Both features make metrics appropriate for science applications.

Random Events 88
- **1.** R   **2.** NR   **3.** R   **4.** NR
- **5.** R   **6.** NR   **7.** NR   **8.** NR

Probability 90
- **1.** 0.25   **2.** 0.1667   **3.** 0.0025
- **4.** 0.75   **5.** 0.0698

More About Probabilities 91
- **1.** 0.1429   **2.** 0.3333   **3.** 0.022
- **4.** Insurance companies base their rates on risk factors. In essence, they use statistical information, based on sampling large populations to determine who is a better risk for insuring. In the case of a smoker versus a nonsmoker, the comparison is easy, since using tobacco products tends to shorten considerably the lives of people. Females also tend to live longer than males. Marriage is also considered by many insurance companies to be a sign of stable habits.
- **5.** 20%
- **6.** Rain is more likely on Thursday.

Data Analysis 92
Answers will vary.

Data 93
All are forms of data.

Answer Key

Answers will vary, but a suggestion is provided for each question.

1. All students enrolled at New Briton Elementary School
2. All people who voted in any of the last 20 local elections
3. Water samples taken from all national parks
4. All rats living within a 500 yard radius of the condemned building
5. All people who belong to the same trade union regardless of the state they live in
6. Radio listeners who have listened to any radio program day or night
7. The members of a local health club who use the swimming pool
8. Scientists who study environmental issues and work only for private companies
9. Crows only
10. Polar bears
11. People who have been hospitalized for a stroke
12. Weather delays only

1. An entire population may be too large for study. That is why smaller samples are chosen.
2. If the sample does not represent the overall population, then the data collected from that sample is of little use.
3. Let us look at a possible survey question as an example: Do you support offshore oil drilling? If this question were asked of oil company executives, the results might be much different than asking a group of people at a local beach. In this case, the sample chosen would influence the results of the survey. There are many ways to structure the way data is collected and analyzed that will influence the results.

1. The 2nd situation is best, since it attempts to find out firsthand why students did not buy a yearbook.
2. The 3rd situation is best. Bicycle shop owners probably know the likes/dislikes of their customers more than the other groups listed.
3. The 3rd situation is best. Ranchers and scientists would certainly have opinions, but firsthand research is the most reliable.
4. The 2nd situation is best. People at a rally probably hold strong opinions, as people working at a factory might also.

Answers will vary.

1. Answers will vary. An interval of 10 is suggested with the first interval being 20 – 29.
2. Answers will vary. An interval of $1.99 is suggested with the first interval being $0.01 – $1.99.

Answer Key

Analyzing Data 103
  I. median—212, mode—201
  2. median—8, mode—2 and 4
  3. median—11, mode—none
  4. median—373, mode—none
  5. median—3, mode—3
  6. median—66, mode—none
  7. median—55, mode—45
  8. median—12, mode—12 and 24

More About Analyzing Data 104
I. 77	**2.** 800	**3.** 15
4. 92.1538	**5.** 3	**6.** 202

I. median	**2.** median	**3.** mean
4. mean		

Using Data to Make Predictions 107
I. extrapolation	**2.** extrapolation
3. interpolation	**4.** extrapolation
5. interpolation	**6.** extrapolation
7. interpolation	**8.** extrapolation

**More About Using Data to
Make Predictions** 108
  I. A good estimate would be 805.
  2. It might be expected that the 2001
    population data will be in the low 400s.
    While this prediction can be made about
    the population, it cannot be verified until
    2001's data is collected.
  3. A good argument could be made that the
    population of trout is declining in this lake,
    and may continue to do so.
  4. Interpolation, since data is known on two
    sides of the predicted figure.
  5. Neither technique yields absolutely
    dependable figures.

More Work with Data 109
  I. A topic for research is decided upon. E
  2. An appropriate sample is selected from the
    population being studied. C
  3. Data is collected for the research project. B
  4. Data is organized in a way that is useful. F
  5. The data is analyzed to determine its
    possible meaning(s). A
  6. The data may then be used for making
    decisions or for making predictions. D

7. F	**8.** T	**9.** T	**10.** T
11. F	**12.** F		

  13. mean 52.692; median 28; mode 28
  14. mean 230; median 200; mode none
  15. mean 44,444; median 2,000; mode none
  16. Her journal entries seem to indicate she
    believes the lake levels are dropping. She
    has used words such as *still* and *only*, as
    well as punctuation to emphasize her
    opinions.
  17. With some data sets, interpolation is a
    viable technique. But this journal is too
    sloppy to hazard a guess with any hopes of
    certainty.
  18. The data would probably be of little use,
    since it was not taken from a sample that
    was representative of the population.
  19. Data that has not been organized lacks a
    systematic way in which it can be
    approached for study.
  20. Each measure tends to look at the data in
    a different light. Sometimes a data set is
    particularly suited to being described by
    one measure but not another, based on its
    characteristics.

Answer Key

Comprehensive Practice 111

1. 0.0833　**2.** $4.62　**3.** $75.00　**4.** 32
5. 1, 2, 4, 5, 8, 10, 20, 40
6. No　　**7.** No　　**8.** 24y　　**9.** 9
10. $3\frac{17}{24}$　**11.** $\frac{2}{3}$　**12.** 25　　**13.** 5
14. 16 cm　　**15.** 415.5 (rounded) sq. ft.
16. 73.5 sq. cm.　　**17.** Yes
18. IV　　**19.** 12.3692
20. $ 56.95　　**21.** 2 hrs., 25 min.
22. Sample
23. A sample that does not represent the intended population will produce erroneous research results.
24. If the data was found to be unreliable, it would have a negative effect on the research produced using the data.
25. They are all useful since they give different views of the data.
26. $150,000　　**27.** 80%
28. 84　　**29.** $\frac{14}{3}$ or $4\frac{2}{3}$
30. 160　**31.** 1, 29　**32.** Yes　**33.** 1:2
34. a pair of right triangles
35. How the shapes will fit together to form an overall pattern depends on the tessellating qualities of the figures.
36. Since the Pythagorean Theorem only applies to right triangles, other techniques must be used for solving triangles that are not right triangles.
37. People who have gotten into a pyramid scheme early have a better mathematical chance of getting their money out before the pyramid collapses.
38. These prime numbers are routinely encountered in many kinds of problems dealing with fractions, division, etc., so it is useful to know them.

Comprehensive Evaluation 115

1. $96.00　**2.** $5,539　**3.** 22　　**4.** No
5. 1, 59　**6.** 6　　**7.** No　　**8.** $\frac{8}{15}$
9. 11:8　**10.** triangular prism　**11.** 20 in.
12. 28 sq. in.　　**13.** 26.8328 cm
14. Yes　**15.** Yes　**16.** 36　**17.** 4.5km
18. No　**19.** 0.01　**20.** 28　**21.** 41.2
22. No
23. The amounts of money coming into a pyramid cannot ultimately sustain it. Also there is usually no true underlying business operation in pyramid schemes other than that of collecting money.
24. That portion of a figure on either side of the line of symmetry will correspond exactly to the portion on the other side.
25. The conditions under which the data was gathered would be of foremost importance.
26. 21.6 gallons　　**27.** centimeters
28. 1:4　　**29.** 120　　**30.** −1
31. −24　　**32.** 19　　**33.** $4,270
34. 5 hours, 50 minutes
35. Major world currencies are valued against each other by financial markets much the same way as stocks. Since a set mathematical relationship exists between currencies, money can be earned simply by charging a percentage fee for the service of making the exchange.
36. Two-dimensional figures can be described in terms of flat areas and plotted on a coordinate plane. Three-dimensional figures exist in space and have volume.
37. Answers will vary. These tools provide a useful way for visually portraying data, often allowing the data to be understood more readily than describing it with text.
38. Answers will vary. While interpolation offers more data parameters to work from when making a prediction, it will not always yield more accurate results.
39. Since the sample gives you a view of the population, it will be a distorted view if an appropriate sample is not obtained.